The French Morane-Saulnier type N 'Bullet'. It was with aircraft such as these that the French pioneered air-to air combat. The type Ns had a forward firing machine gun, but it was not synchronised with the revolutions of the propeller. The French devised a system using steel plates bolted to the wooden propeller blades, the idea being that at least some would get through! This proved to be a very effective system, until the Germans shot one down and went one better. An interrupter gear was designed by Anthony Fokker who installed a synchronised machine gun on his Fokker Eindekkers (pages 26/27). Thus air-to-air combat during WW 1 started in earnest. Here display pilot Jonathon Whaley returns from an airshow in a type N from Tony Bianchi's 'The Blue Max Collection'.

OPPOSITE *The German Junkers JU 52* transport of WW 2. This classic tri-motor saw extensive service as an airliner in the 1930s flying with Lufthansa, where it carried around 75 per cent of all the airlines' European passengers. During WW 2 it was the mainstay of the Luftwaffe's transport fleet, where it played a vital role in the developement of Germany's airborne assault techniques. The JU 52 was affectionately known as Tante Ju (Auntie Ju), or Iron Annie.

AIRSHOW

The World's Classic Aircraft on Display

JON DAVISON

Virgin

First published in Great Britain in 1992 by
Virgin Books
an imprint of Virgin Publishing Ltd
338 Ladbroke Grove
London W10 5AH

A catalogue record for this book is available from the British Library

ISBN 0 86369 509 4

Printed and bound by Singapore National Printers Ltd.

Produced by:
Inspired Images (Oxford) Ltd, Regal Court, London Road, Oxford OX3 9AU
Tel: 0865 741296. Fax: 0865 64276

Concept, Design & Photography: Jon Davison

Text & Narratives: Molly O'Loughlin White, Jon Davison & Flt Lt Ken Delve

Editorial Research: Molly O'Loughlin White & Jenny Anne Oliver

Studio Production: Jerry Burman

Production Executive: Barry Roberts

Publisher: Robert Shreeve

All photographs by Jon Davison except pages 10 (bottom) & 102, both by Lindsay Peacock and page 55 (top) Richard Leonard.

Photographs:
PAGE 1. *Lockheed T-33, the two seat trainer version of the P-80 Shooting Star.*
THIS PAGE: Top *De Havilland Dove*. Bottom *DH Rapide*.
OPPOSITE: *The Lockheed U2/TR1 high altitude reconnaissance aircraft.*
BACKGROUND IMAGE: *1930s Hawker Fury.*

CONTENTS

FOREWORD

For as long as I can remember, flying has been a passion of mine. More than that, an obsession. To be at the controls of a thundering warbird was one of my wilder dreams.

Success as a professional musician enabled me to turn that dream into a reality, and I eventually became an air display pilot. I now fly and rub shoulders with some of the finest pilots in the world. As a relative novice to airshow flying I am now beginning to learn what people mean by 'real flying'.

I like to think that airshows promote aviation. They encourage the young to get involved and salute the achievements and courage of older generations.

When I'm flying my Harvard I am constantly aware of its history and feel a genuine sense of responsibility, not only to keep it safe and well maintained, but to share the experience of it with as many people as possible. This is surely what airshows are for, and it is what this book is for. *Airshow* is an admirable piece of work and I am very flattered to have been asked by Jon Davison and his team to write the foreword for it.

An air display is not just a demonstration of a flying machine and the skill of its pilot. It is a display of that pilot's love and passion for flying itself. A display of history, elegance and power. A smoke-trail signature of perfection.

A well-flown display is a work of art, and the aeroplane, surely, is the most beautiful machine ever created.

This book captures the magic of man and machine working together. It is a fascinating look at the airshow world and I thoroughly recommend it to you all.

Gary Numan

Rock musician Gary Numan's *distinctive 'electronic' music has given him that all important edge. This has allowed him to build up an extremely dedicated following of fans and from this position he has been able to shrug off the passing fashions of the music industry. In his twelve year career Gary has had 30 chart singles including 2 Number Ones, with* Are Friends Electric? *and* Cars.

Author's Note

Like a lot of books that have some sort of author's preface, *Airshow* was also going to have one. After seeing Molly's introduction and Gary's foreword, I decided that there was not a lot more that I could add to their words, as they have set the scene for the images and narrative. At length I decided that if I were to add a classic poem that to me portrayed the beauty of flight, it would have to be the immortal words of John Gillespie Magee, Jr. He was a pilot in the Royal Canadian Air Force and was killed in action in 1941. He was 19 years old when he wrote *High Flight*, which to my mind says it all.

Jon Davison 1992

High Flight

*Oh, I have slipped the surly bonds of Earth
And danced the skies on laughter-silvered wings;
Sunward I've climbed and joined the tumbling mirth
Of sun-split clouds – and done a hundred things
You have not dreamed of – wheeled and soared and swung
High in the sunlit silence; hovering there,
I've chased the shouting wind along, and flung
My eager craft through footless halls of air.*

*Up, up the long, delirious burning blue
I've topped the wind-swept heights with easy grace
Where never lark, or even eagle ever flew –
And, while with silent lifting mind I've trod
The high untrespassed sanctity of space,
Put out my hand and touched the face of God.*

John Gillespie Magee, Jr.

INTRODUCTION

BACKGROUND IMAGE *Curtiss P-40 Kittyhawk*
BELOW *De Havilland Mosquito.*
BOTTOM *Douglas A-26 Invader.*

"Ladies and gentlemen – from the right . . . the Vulcan . . ."

Ten thousand pairs of eyes (and more) swivel and follow an apparition of delta-winged fury as the aircraft roars past the crowdline and climbs into sun and cloud still mottled with rainbow smoke from a departing display team.

It's a typical summer's day airshow scene that can be repeated over almost the whole world as one pilot or team follows another, displaying flicks and rolls, manoeuvres and co-ordination, pushing each aircraft to extremes of its frontier and thrilling those earthbound mortals below with their courage and skills.

But why are they here, these folk with their feet firmly on the ground? They are here because an airshow is the gateway to aviation, shared among everyone. They are here because they equate freedom with flight, but most of all for the sheer joy of flight, for some short while, if only in mutual dreams.

They are also here to admire the endeavours of those who build and restore old warriors from the two world wars, vintage aircraft which helped preserve the freedom which we enjoy today. After years of sacrificed leisure by teams of devotees they are now immaculate and proudly flown, each one with its own following.

We are fortunate to have such diversity of airshows from Farnborough International, Paris, Singapore or Oshkosh to the precision operated military tattos and shows of air forces and armies, to 'twilight' flying displays of museum treasures or highly popular flying association fly-ins.

Aeroplanes come closer to being 'alive' than any other man-made machine. In his pictures Jon Davison has captured that 'life' and the charisma and unique characteristics of each aircraft – and the magical madness of action and angles and light in the changing skies of the flying airshow scene.

This book begins with what is to every fledgling pilot the true start of a new life in the air – going solo. Some of the traditional training aircraft which also show their paces to the public are depicted. The next chapter is about classic pistons, forty-two pages of well-loved and well-known favourites on the airshow circuit, from the B-17 Flying Fortress, Spitfire and Hurricane to the P-51 Mustang, Grumman WW 2 and post-war Grumman fighters.

The scene changes in Chapter 3 to the 'fast and furious' combat aircraft, most of them still in military service today. These are the display stars of the airshow circuit and the photos show them in action, thrilling the crowds with the wonders of ultra-modern technology while the commentator pointedly reminds them that 'for real' they are actively protecting our heritage, that each exciting manoeuvre results from the requirement to seek, strike and avoid. Many shone in the Gulf and Falklands conflicts.

Chapter 4 depicts the 'heavies' of the aviation world, from tankers and bombers to the larger 'jumbo' freighters (including the gigantic A-225 'Dream'). Each one fills the viewfinder with its own bulky photogenic presence. Helicopters are not forgotten, with part of a chapter devoted to the large Russian helicopters and a two-page show of helicopter display teams. Built for war, both fixed-wing and helicopter 'heavies' are bringing relief with peace-time missions in areas of disaster.

The last chapters of the book are devoted to display teams with some rare shots of the most famous international teams in action. Finally, some of the work going on in bringing old treasures 'back to life' is depicted.

Many aficionados, pilots, air crew, ground crew, passengers and show visitors have contributed to the text, recalling favourite and not so favourite moments, exciting and funny experiences, or just traits that intrigue.

Browse through these pages and relive the smell of cut grass and clean metal and fuel, the music of Merlins and jets, the wind and rain and never to be forgotten blissful summer days – and, most of all, the freedom and joy of flight. It's all here in *Airshow*.

Molly O'Loughlin White

Breaking with their single-engined heritage, Grumman's F7F Tigercat was too late to see action during WW 2 but did see action in the Korean War as a night fighter. The Tigercat had exceptional power, speed and manoeuvrability.

OVERLEAF **The classic and purposeful lines of the Hawker Fury,** the last biplane fighter to see service with the Royal Air Force. As such it was operational from the late 1920s through to the mid 1930s. The Fury also saw service with the air forces of Spain, Persia and Yugoslavia. The Fury had an excellent climb rate, and was used primarily as an interceptor. Here the Fury is flown by display pilot Jonathon Whaley, on a test flight after a major overhaul by Tony Bianchi's Personal Plane Services. The Fury now resides in Belgium and is owned and operated by biplane collector Robert Landuyt.

INSET **The Consolidated Vultee BT-13 Valiant trainer.** *The 'Vibrator' as it was generally known introduced students to R/T instrument flying and, like the Texan, gave students the first taste of a machine with the qualities of a fighter.*

RIGHT **Piper Warrior.** *This excellent light trainer has become a mainstay in civil airliner pilot training.*

CHAPTER 1

GOING SOLO

The time has come. The moment of truth that you both long for and dread, when your instructor unfastens his seatbelt and walks away from the aircraft with a gentle good luck tap-tap on the fuselage. You taxi towards the holding point in a state of bewilderment and exhilaration, stopping only to fumble through power checks. At the hold, two aircraft sail in to land and the seconds seem like eternity before you are cleared for take off. Full power, and the little trainer is rolling down the runway. The Air Speed Indicator shows rotate speed. A backward nudge of the control column and you're airborne. Simple aerodynamics, but a never failing moment of pure magic! Climbing away from the mortal world, you're on your first solo. A once-in-a-lifetime occasion in any pilot's life.

You expect to feel scared but instead there is just a mild sensation of surprise that here you are, alone in the sky with the aeroplane and the thrum of its pushy engine driving the little propeller – and it is actually flying for YOU!

There is the calm voice of the controller answering your early downwind call. There is much to do, keeping the aircraft in balance and on course, at the correct height and speed, watching for other aircraft and the checks of instruments and controls, for wayward thoughts.

In no time you are on base leg, preparing to land. Reduce power, trim for descent, flaps. A descending turn, and there is the friendly runway. The trainer, an old faithful that has carried innumerable budding pilots on their first solos, sails in and lands kindly. You taxi back to the flying school on cloud nine.

Inside the clubhouse your instructor will tell you that it's just another landmark in any pilot's training. But the old hands are smiling, each one remembering his own first solo. And they know that, tonight, the beer is on you!

Whether a pilot starts his flying training on a Chipmunk or Tiger Moth, Texan or 'Vibrator', or one of the civil light trainers, that first solo is just the same. And whether he ends up the captain of a jumbo jet, a military ace or display pilot, the basic training for the PPL is the start – in fact many military pilots begin with a flying scholarship at the local club.

The single-engined trainers each have an individual character, all their own. Like mettlesome horses they will boss you if you do not master them. But handle them with firmness and tact and they are responsive and forgiving.

Fly – and you are responsible for your own destiny. Refuse to accept that fact – and you do not have long to live, for the penalty for a bad mistake is – death. Accept that you never stop learning in the air and you are halfway to your own survival.

ABOVE *The De Havilland Chipmunk tandem seat primary trainer.* This 40-year-old machine will no doubt still be providing air cadets with their first taste of powered flight as the twenty-first century dawns.

The De Havilland D. H. 82 Tiger Moth *basic trainer entered service with the RAF in 1932. This superb machine served throughout WW 2 and is still flying in many countries today. The Diamond Nine display team and their Tiger Moths are a regular sight at airshows around the UK.*

"I do not think any pilot has experienced the real joy of flying unless he or she has flown the Tiger Moth. It will be remembered as one of the world's most famous training aircraft and was an RAF trainer for over 15 years. During the war most RAF pilots were trained on Tiger Moths. Over 4,000 were built for the RAF and another 3,000 were made in Canada, Australia and New Zealand.

I learnt to fly in the Tiger Moth in 1956. I was then a member of the Oxford Aeroplane Club which had four, all beautifully painted in pristine white with two blue lines along the whole length of the fuselage.

I especially liked the compass arrangement which was on the floor between your knees, and you merely had to line up the two white lines either side of the needle and then read off the heading on the white line.

The main problem was reading your map on a cross country flight. You had to hold the control column between your knees in order to get a closer look and prevent it blowing over the side of the cockpit. This happened to me on one flight and I had to fly purely by ground reference and follow the River Thames back to the airport."

Peter Wilkins, veteran pilot

TIGER MOTH

The French Morane-Saulnier 230 was designed as an advanced trainer to give students the look and feel of a contemporary fighter. The 230 saw service with the French Air Force and Navy from the late 1920s through to WW 2.

"**T**his is a unique airplane, both in appearance and to fly. It is a direct descendant of WW 1 but with a good 1930s powerplant and more modern systems. It is beautifully engineered and thoroughly usable providing you have a dedicated ground crew. From a pilot's point of view, few airplanes can give quite the pleasure of flying that this machine does.

In the Morane 230 you sit a long way down the fuselage, and the aircraft has a steep ground angle so consequently when the tail is raised for take-off or lowered for landing, you travel up and down quite a distance. Directional stability on the ground is poor and is not helped by the lack of brakes. The Morane is powerful and will perform all aerobatics classically, including outside loops and flick rolls. The rate of roll is incredibly slow and difficult and requires a lot of practice, but similar Moranes won international aerobatic contests before WW 2.

In 1939 most MS-230s were impounded by the Luftwaffe, who crashed them all within a very short period in landing accidents. Now only three are flying in the world.

As is the way of the collector's world, the appeal of macho expensive fighters – and only having practical experience of your own country's airplanes – has overshadowed some of the most perfect and desirable aircraft ever made. The Morane-Saulnier 230 is one of these."

Tony Bianchi, 'The Blue Max Collection'

MORANE 230

ABOVE *Due to its Japanese 'Zero' lookalike characteristics,* the AT-6 does tend to end up trailing smoke as the 'victim'.

AT-6 TEXAN

"Like untold thousands of pilots during the war, I trained in the AT-6 Texan, though over in the UK you call them Harvards, I think. When I first saw one it looked awesome: after time on the PT-17 and BT-13, the Texan really looked like a fighter, and by Jesus it was loud. I have seen many fellow recruits bust their kites in all sorts of incredible situations, and then walk away. God knows how but they did, though some of course didn't. On one occasion after I had spent some time on the Texan, I was merrily heading back to base after doing some aerobatics, when I thought I felt my instructor wanting to take control and because I had a problem with my ears, I couldn't hear what he was saying. I thought, 'Okay, so he wants control, well, he's got it', so I just took my hands off the stick and relaxed.

We had a very smooth landing, no bumps at all, and I thought, 'Well, I've got a lot to learn yet!' After we taxied in and stopped my instructor said, 'That was one of the best landings I've had the pleasure of experiencing.' I thought, 'You smug sonofabitch.' He then said, 'I think you're on your own now, you made one hell of a landing.' Well, I sure as darn didn't land the thing, and if it wasn't my instructor . . . I still don't know to this day; I think I was too shocked to ask him. Anyway I got through and went on to P38 Lightnings . . . and I'm still alive!"

Lorne Krantz, airshow spectator and ex-USAF fighter pilot

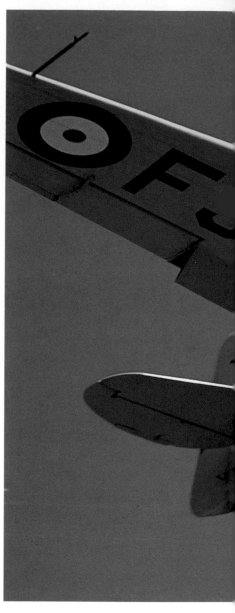

ABOVE *The North American AT-6/5NJ Texan* (Harvard) trained more allied pilots than any other aircraft. It was an advanced trainer with the look, feel and size of a fighter, and had a maximum speed of just over 200 mph. Its characteristic propeller 'scream' is due to the tips of the blade travelling at trans-sonic speeds.
RIGHT *This Texan, an SNJ-3,* is one of the oldest flying Texans. She first saw service with the RCAF in the 1940s, and was bought by the Italian Air Force in the late 50s. Eventually being retired in 1974, she was brought to the UK in 1981, was ready for her airshow debut in 1987, and is now flying with the Harvard Formation Team at North Weald. She is painted in the colours of a SNJ-3 of the US Navy.

The Yakovlev Yak 11 *was one of the Soviet Union's most successful post-war trainers.*

"I flew the Yak for a few years. It was the first one to be seen in the UK and was rescued from Cyprus after a crash and brought to Britain where we restored it. It was a classic, beautiful machine to fly, absolutely brilliant, well made and reliable, a superb trainer. The Yak will quite happily cruise at 220kts, dive to 325kts, and you can achieve with that, I think, as good an aerobatic and airshow performance as you can with any other WW 2 aircraft.

It has got a fast rate of roll and it's fairly small, so it looks impressive. We always used to start an airshow with the Yak by climbing to 6,000ft somewhere close to the field and just roll it on its back, then gently pull up and do two vertical rolls. The late Neil Williams was the real maestro of the Yak and I have tried to emulate his style at flying as much as possible. I don't think there are many WW 2 aircraft apart from the Sea Fury or Bearcat that you can do these sort of manoeuvres with, bearing in mind that the Yak has only 800bhp. The only thing I would say about it is that it is not an aircraft to take liberties with. It has got very small wings and if you pull tight in a turn and the speed gets low, it will flick on you."

Tony Bianchi, display pilot

YAK 11

CHAPTER 2

CLASSIC PISTONS

All the aircraft in this chapter are yesterday's warbirds, machines that were designed to defend and attack. They were built in greater numbers than any other type of flying machine the world has ever seen, or no doubt will ever see again.

Created to carry men and munitions high above the earth and to operate from locations as diverse as desert and jungle airstrips, carriers and even the ocean itself, these flying machines were the catapults and bows and arrows of another century.

Today many of these finely crafted machines have been lovingly restored to flying condition after being salvaged from scrap heaps and from graves in the very places where they fell . . . tropical jungles, deserts, mountains and sea beds.

These restored warbirds represent some of the machines that took part in the most calamitous conflicts ever witnessed. They are a memorial to the tens of thousands of young men and women who flew and died in them.

At the end of hostilities in 1918 and 1945, vast armadas of aircraft were either unceremoniously melted down, sold for scrap or purchased by private owners. Others were put into service pioneering routes for fledgling airlines. The ones that have made it through to the 1990s are few and far between. The rare birds seen today, such as the Lancaster, BF-109G and Hellcat might be one of only two left flying in the world. They appear as the only visual and audible proof that these once proud machines ever existed at all, out of the tens of thousands that were produced. It is through the bitter lessons learnt from the experience provided by the classic pistons that aviation has become the high tech industry it is today.

Boeing B-17 Flying Fortress in formation with a Republic P-47 Thunderbolt. The P-47 often acted as an escort fighter to the B-17 on the long daylight raids over Northern Europe during WW 2.

INSET ***Considered by many to be Germany's finest WW 1 fighter,*** *the Fokker D.V11 was an extremely strong, manoeuvrable and well armed machine. With a top speed of 120mph it was far superior to most fighters of the period.*

MAIN PICTURE ***The dreaded German Fokker E of WW 1*** *(the 'E' stood for Eindekker, or monoplane). This aircraft was the first flying machine to be produced with a synchronised machine gun firing between the propeller blades. The Eindekker had a top speed of only 80mph but it made up for this with its superior armament. During the 6 months that this machine dominated the skies, the allies coined the term 'Fokker scourge'. It was so successful that by the end of 1915 the French had abandoned their bombing missions due to the heavy losses incurred. Today this Eindekker is owned and flown by Tony Bianchi who has piloted many of the aerial sequences in the 'Indiana Jones' series of films.*

FOKKER

"The big problem with the Eindekker is that the wings are very flexible. This aircraft, a replica, has ailerons and not warping wings as original. However, when you deflect the ailerons, the wings go the opposite way, so alas we have warping wings!

You get a strange roll reversal in turbulence, most uncomfortable and dangerous – in fact a bloody monster is created, so we only fly in good conditions. On a calm summer's evening it is difficult to believe you are flying the same aeroplane, it is quite a joy.

To imagine Immelmann making his famous combat turn is also quite difficult to believe, but pilots are not what they used to be, I suppose.

Once in the early seventies I was flying the Eindekker back from an airshow where we had been doing a dog fight sequence. In those days we had gas-operated machine guns and had clip on smoke canisters. About five minutes out from the airshow I noticed a couple in a corn field 'enjoying themselves', I rattled the guns a few times and dived and turned around them at about 300 feet. After one 360° turn I noticed them rushing around this field trying to put out a fire from a smoke pot that had accidentally fallen off the aircraft. The Eindekker is a lot of fun to fly."

Tony Bianchi, 'The Blue Max Collection'

RIGHT *The Fokker DR 1 Triplane* (DR = Drie, meaning 3) of WW 1. It
was with a machine like this that Germany's 'Red Knight', Manfred
Freiherr von Richthofen, scored many of his 80 aerial victories. He was
the highest scoring ace of the war.

The Sopwith Camel entered service in June 1917. Even though it made a late entrance into WW 1 the Camel claimed 3,000 victories, more than any other flying machine or any other nation during the war. Here the Camel is piloted by Jonathon Whaley from Tony Bianchi's 'The Blue Max Collection' (pages 2, 9, 27). The collection's vintage aircraft have appeared in many major motion pictures, including: The Blue Max, Aces High, High Road to China and the 'Indiana Jones' series of films.

"That's the worst aeroplane I've ever flown!
A surprisingly normal reaction from pilots having flown the Sopwith Camel for the first time. You would think that Britain's most famous WW 1 fighter was as glorious to fly as all the books say, but it's not! But it grows on you. It has an excellent performance, turns tight, climbs well and keeps you busy. Our aircraft was built by Talmantz Aviation for the film *The Great Waldo Pepper*, so it has the benefit of a radial engine and a steel-tube fuselage. The Camel's original construction was pretty frightening, the engine and mounting plate being held in by piano wire and turnbuckles. In theory it is possible to lose the whole lot off the front leaving you sitting with your feet out in the breeze!

Pilots not experienced in engine handling had accidents in Camels. The clerget required delicate mixture adjustments; even with a take-off and climb through 300 feet the engine could misfire and stop if not set correctly. The other peculiarity was that the aircraft had a very short coupled fuselage, so to improve manoeuvrability they put the fuel tank behind the pilot, so making an aft centre of gravity. With a more than quarter-full tank the Camel is impossible – unstable, and quite difficult to control in turbulent conditions.

Saying that, the Camel is a delight to fly when it's warm and calm."

Camel display pilot, 'The Blue Max Collection'

SOPWITH CAMEL

The unmistakable lines of the Beech 18 'Expeditor'. The production of the Beech, or C-45 (in its military role), lasted for 32 years with a total of 6,326 examples. This particular aircraft is painted in the colours of a C-45 of the USAAC. The C-45 served with Allied air forces throughout the world during WW 2.

"It's a great tutor – marvellous to fly and very stable but keeps you on your toes. A typical 1930s trainer. Our Beech Expeditor N5063N is a major part of the Harvard Formation Team. Besides acting as 'Mother Ship' and team transport it also plays an important part in the team's displays. It is flown by John Webb with the Harvards and also on its own.

A weekend 'squadron raid' with the team on Perigueux in France was tremendous for Anglo-Franco-Spanish entente. We met up with another Beech and a team of 18 Harvards from Madrid. We were entertained to a magnificent banquet.

I rescued our Beech from Duxford where it had blown into a fence. An American friend worked on it and got it flying in the record time of five weeks. With new engines it now has a working life of 15 years. It is painted in the markings of HB275, an Expeditor serving in India during WW 2 which suffered undercarriage problems after many heavy landings and was struck off charge in 1945.

The Beech 18 (or C-45 as the military version was designated) was given many names, not all of them complimentary – Expeditor, Kansas, Navigator, Twin Harvard, Wichita Wobbler, Bug Basher and Explorer, but basically the design remained the same.

It is a remarkable achievement that, having first flown in 1937, it continued to be built for 32 years until 1969, a record that will probably never be beaten by any other type in history. The twin engined all metal aeroplane was designed with a twin tailplane because Walter Beech decided that 'the modern twin-engined airplane should have a rudder behind each engine for optimum control'."

Anthony Hutton, Beech operator, Harvard Formation Team

BEECH C-45

Boeing's famous B-17, nicknamed 'Flying Fortress' by the press when it first came into service in the late 1930s. Boeing liked the name and subsequently registered it for their new bomber. The largest number of B-17s to be launched at a target was an incredible 1,400, on Christmas Eve 1944.

We were at an airshow in Liege, Belgium, once and had a Sea Fury, a Spitfire, a Mustang and a B25 Mitchell there. We planned out a display with the other pilots, did a formation and break and so on, and at the end Harry Van Dijk of Vintage Aircraft Promotions, a Dutchman, came up to us with his father. His father, he told us, had come because he wanted to hear the sounds of the old aeroplanes, because to him the sounds of the Wright Cyclones, the Pratt & Whitneys and the Merlins, were the sounds of freedom.

That sort of thing stops you in your tracks; it brings a lump to your throat. That's the kind of thing this aeroplane does to people. It does it to us, the pilots, because we can use our imagination and think what it must have been like to fly these planes in the war, but it does it to the specta-tors because many of them actually lived that moment.

Then we get the odd amusing incident, like the time we were coming back from Sweden last year and were transferring from Copenhagen control to Bremen control, and my co-pilot called up and said 'Golf Bravo Echo Delta Foxtrot, a B17 from Sonderberg to Norwich, VFR, request clearance to transit your airspace' – and the air control came back and said 'Oh, I understand that's a formation of B17s en route!'– and Jim said 'Oh no, only one this time', and the controller said 'OK, in that case you're clear to transit – there won't be any flak today'. "

Captain Keith Sissons, B-17 'Sally B'

B-17 FLYING FORTRESS

Boeing B-17G Flying Fortress 'Sally B', the star of the motion picture Memphis Belle, *is a regular participant at major airshows in the UK and Europe and is owned by Elly Salingboe of B-17 Preservation Ltd.*
LEFT *Sally B's chief pilot Captain Keith Sissons winds up the Wright Cyclones for another airshow at Duxford.*

"We hadn't had a full crew before on the Sally B, until the *Memphis Belle* film which was then mainly actors, and then several of them were actually our engineers acting as gunners assisted by armament technicians from the film company. What really surprised us then was when the guns were fired, the amount of shaking and vibrating that went on was incredible as was the smell of cordite. The racket, smell, vibration and then imagine being shot at as well with all the confusion, terrifying!

During the war these chaps would leave their billets early in the morning, get airborne, fly away from the relative normality of England to deliver their loads over Germany, and then, if they survived, come back in the evening and go off to the pub for a drink with the local farmers who had probably had a very ordinary day, and the next day go off to battle again!

So whereas I fly around the shows and it's a lot of fun, when I fly over somewhere like Maddingly Cemetery, as I've just done, I like to make a personal salute to those chaps who died in the war. It's been particularly moving to fly across there with a P-51 Mustang on the wing-tip; that is very satisfying to do and it's nice to have an aeroplane flying the airshow circuit that means something rather special to people.

I remember flying across East Anglia one day with Chris Bevan, my co-pilot, and we were coming back over the old B-17 base at Thorpe Abbots. It was a lovely day like this, and as we flew, Chris called out the names of all the old airfields we were passing – you can still see them from the air – and he said, 'You know, Keith, being in this aeroplane and flying across East Anglia is like flying in a ghost ship' – and I thought that summed it up in a way."

Captain Keith Sissons, B-17 'Sally B'

B-17 FLYING FORTRESS

The Republic P-47 Thunderbolt was produced in more numbers than any other American fighter during WW 2: production totalled a staggering 15,500 examples. The Thunderbolt or 'Jug' served with the air forces of the United States, Mexico, the Free French, the Soviet Union, Brazil and Great Britain. The P-47 was the heaviest single-engined fighter of the war, yet was equal to any machine it met, capable of outdiving the BF109 and FW190 and overtaking them in level flight.

"One of the great fighter aircraft of WW 2, the 'Jug' has seldom been given the attention it deserves, being overshadowed by other contemporary types such as the Mustang. It saw extensive service with the USAF, operationally. It performed excellent work as a fighter and fighter-bomber, proving adept at close air support, planting its bombs with great accuracy – much to the delight of the hard-pressed on the ground .

The performance and agility of the aircraft belied its size and ungainly shape. Once in the air the Jug was a real high-class performer. One of the biggest problems when our squadron first re-equipped was accidents on take-off; the P-47 was a real handful with its very powerful Double-Wasp engine. The large clear bubble canopy gave a good all-round view, a great advantage in a fight – as was the top speed of over 400 mph. It was a pleasure to go up with an aircraft that gave you the edge; power, performance, and the stopping power of eight half-inch machine-guns."

Ex P-47 pilot

P-47 THUNDERBOLT

SPITFIRE

"My first flight in G-FIRE was from Staverton, where she had been left with suspected fouled plugs, to Elstree aerodrome where she was based at the time of Spencer Flack's ownership. I had not flown a Griffon engined 'Spit' for over two years and never into such a short runway as at Elstree. My intention was to make three circuits at Staverton prior to heading East, to get the feel of her before putting her onto Elstree's short runway. The first take-off gave me the biggest surprise – 65 on the clock – start to ease her off, straight into a mild buffet. What's this? Stall warning – at this speed?

By this time the powerful Griffon was getting the aircraft's skirts up and the problem no longer existed. I was still pondering when I came round for the first roller. Then, as I started to peg the approach speed, I spotted it. The ASI was in mph, not knots. No wonder she was protesting on take-off.

G-FIRE is beautifully equipped with modern avionics – twin VHF, a KNS80 that can store 4 VORs and a transponder. 'Magic', says Pete, 'shan't get lost, or wouldn't if I knew how to use it!' I later tackled Spencer: 'Why don't you have the ASI changed, Spence? The aircraft is equipped up to the ying yang with avionics, all reading out in knots, and you have this ASI in mph?' 'Ah well', said Spencer, 'you have to keep the aircraft authentic.' There's no answer to that!"

Pete Thorn, display pilot

The Supermarine Spitfire is remembered above all for its part in the Battle of Britain. *Although the Hurricane flew in far greater numbers and shot down more aircraft, the Spitfire, due to its classical elliptical wing, had a grace and beauty that secured its place in history. The Spitfire was the brainchild of R.J. Mitchell, who had been developing a series of high-speed Supermarine seaplanes for the International Schneider Trophy races during the late 1920s and early 30s. The ultimate design was the S.6B which won the trophy for Great Britain in 1931.*

BELOW & BOTTOM LEFT **Spitfire ML407 is one of the few two-seat trainers left flying,** in this case a MK 1X. ML407 was converted to a trainer after the war and served with the Irish Air Corps untill the late 1960s. A sister MK 1X (ML417) is also to be seen on the airshow circuit, although she has now been converted to a single seater (previous page, top right, wearing invasion stripes). Only 20 MK 1Xs were converted to trainers.

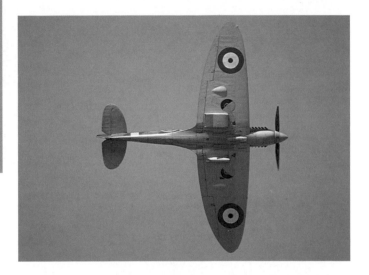

Two versions of the Messerschmitt BF-109G, one of Germany's most outstanding fighters of WW 2. ABOVE *An ex-Spanish Air Force HA.112 Buchon,* a licence built BF 109G by CASA, but fitted with a Rolls Royce Merlin (the same as the Spitfire).
RIGHT, OPPOSITE & BELOW *The real thing! A BF-109G-2,* restored over the last 20 years by the RAF under Flt Lt Russ Snadden. It is the only Daimler Benz powered Messerschmitt in the world.

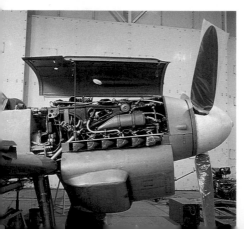

MESSERSCHMITT BF-109G

"Our Messerschmitt 109G is the only German built model in the world still flying. It has an interesting history. Built in Leipzig in mid-1942 it joined JG77 Fighter Group and was flown via Italy to North Africa. By the end of October 1942 it became the first of its series to be captured, in a damaged condition, at Gambut Airfield by the Royal Australian Air Force. They made it airworthy and by 1943 it was seeing action in RAF colours in Cairo, Palestine and south of Suez.

It was eventually shipped to the UK, to 1426 Enemy Aircraft Flight at Collyweston, Lincs, and then put into storage. By 1972 it was just a robbed hulk and our task since then has been to rebuild it with bits from all over the world. It's been a lot of hard work by dedicated people with long-suffering wives!

It first flew at RAF Benson in March 1991 and is now based at Duxford, to be operated by the Imperial War Museum for the next three years. During test flying the pilots built up a great affection for the aircraft. The display includes slow rolls and a semi-loop, rolling off the top. The chief pilot, Air Vice Marshal John Allison, and second pilot Sqn Ldr Dave Southward both say it's delightful to fly, especially at low speed.

The BF-109G was first flown in 1935 and manufactured in greater numbers than any other WW 2 aircraft, believed to be 33,000. The first aircraft off the production line actually had a Rolls Royce Kestrel engine. There was an early production line in Spain where it was named the 'Buchon' ('deep chested pigeon' in Spanish) and powered with Merlin engines. As well as serving with the Luftwaffe, it flew with the Condor Legion in the Spanish Civil War and the air forces of Switzerland, Finland, Czechoslovakia and Israel."

Russ Snadden, project leader of the Messerschmitt 109G restoration team

The Last
of the Many!

ABOVE ***Designed in 1933 by Sir Sidney Camm and his team,*** *the Hawker Hurricane first flew in 1935. During the Battle of Britain the Hurricane destroyed more enemy machines than the sum total of all other defences (aircraft & AA guns).*
LEFT ***The last of the many!*** *A Hurricane Mk 11C.*

"I have had many happy sorties with the Hurricanes in the Battle of Britain Memorial Flight. However, my first memorable occasion in the Hurricane was a 'non-flying' event! We stopped overnight at Northolt, en route for the Jersey Show.

Next morning there was a stiff breeze and as we taxied out to the runway the aircraft were doing their best to weathercock into wind. We were very conscious of the possibility of brake fade. The Hurricane was particularly prone if you were over zealous with the brakes. As I negotiated a 90^0 bend in the perimeter track, with the wind intent on making the Hurricane turn through considerably more, to my horror the port undercarriage collapsed. Two of the three propeller blades hit the concrete and we lost four inches off both.

You don't have to use a lot of imagination to know how I felt. The undercarriage lever was in the down position and I could only assume a structural failure. What made it worse, the duty fireman arrived with all his gear and asked: 'Is this a practice, sir?' He was lucky to get away with his life."

Pete Thorn, Battle of Britain Memorial Flight display pilot

HURRICANE

P-51 MUSTANG

The Mustang, compared with many other fighters of the WW 2 era, shows few signs of its late 1930s design and construction. In most respects it is in fact representative of the jet age of over-engineered quality. Unlike, for example, the MK9 Spitfire which is mistakenly compared with the P-51. The British fighter is more of a sports car, with direct parentage to the 1930s biplane age in design and construction, and even in flight characteristics in some areas, whereas the P-51 was more like a Lincoln Continental.

The P-51 has several tons of fuel capacity, whereas the Spitfire is struggling with a 1½ hour flight time. It has comfort, a high speed cruise and never overheats on the ground.

On the downside from a Spitfire pilot's viewpoint, the P-51 has a slow and disappointing take off and climb rate. It requires a strong right arm to make impressive aerobatics if they are anything other than basic manoeuvres. It also requires an airfield of greater dimensions than the Spitfire.

All of these points, though, are quite trivial when you consider the Mustang's long service career around the world, and even until quite recently in a combat role. This career is a testimony to the great success of this remarkable fighter."

P-51 through the eyes of a Spitfire pilot

The P-51 Mustang was one of the greatest, if not the best piston engined fighter of WW 2. The P-51 started reaching operational squadrons in 1943 and its endurance meant that it could provide fighter cover for the daylight raids all the way to the target and back again. This substantially reduced the horrendous losses being suffered by the B-17 and B-24 bombers. Today the P-51 is one of the most numerous of the restored WW 2 warbirds.

"The 'bent wing bastard from Connecticut' is what pilots called this bird when they first started flying it. I don't know if they do any more. Its huge 13ft-diameter propeller meant that it had to have cranked wings which was an ingenious design solution. This got around the problem of the undercarriage being too long and also meant that the propeller blades didn't chew up the deck on landing.

We found the Corsair to be a great fighter and we used it a lot in the Pacific when we were based in Espiritu Santo. Because of its speed, climb rate and huge propeller, if you ever ran out of ammo, you could always fly up behind your target and saw his tail surfaces off. I think it is still the most numerous aircraft that has ever been employed in the service of the New Zealand government."

F4U-1 pilot, ex-Royal New Zealand Air Force

The Chance Vought F4U Corsair shipboard and landbased fighter (of the US Navy and Marine Corps). This odd looking aircraft was the first fighter to exceed 400mph in level flight and became one of the finest naval fighters of WW 2.
LEFT *This particular Corsair, an F4U-5*, is painted in the colours of the Royal New Zealand Airforce, who during WW 2 received 419 F4U-1Ds. The Royal Navy received 2,012 Corsairs.

OVERLEAF *Goodyear FG1-D Corsair* from 'The Old Flying Machine Company'.

F4U CORSAIR

The Consolidated PBY-5A Catalina was the most important flying boat of WW 2. It had an enormous range and could patrol the oceans for very long periods, and because of this it was able to rescue thousands of downed airmen. The 'Cat' could also be armed with torpedoes and other weapons.

The only hiccup we had when John Watts and I flew the Catalina from Johannesburg to the UK was at Marseilles when it refused to start. It was in February and it obviously objected to the freezing cold weather. The trip took just under a week – 48 hours' flying time. We were two hours behind schedule! Not bad considering the distance and that it was like a dirty old tramp steamer, airworthy but a bit dilapidated.

Our route was via Lusaka, Nairobi, Khartoum, Alexandria, Palermo, Cagliari (where we picked up Paul Warren Wilson whose company Plane Sailing Air Displays now operates the Catalina), Marseilles, Paris and Manston where we were escorted in by a Nimrod.

It hadn't been operated on water for years but the following year after tests at Trondheim it starred in the film *48 Grosvenor Street*. Since then it's landed on odd waterways including the Thames at Barking. It taxied through the Thames Barrier and Tower Bridge was opened to allow it to continue to the Pool of London, an hour and a quarter's taxiing time and back to take off again. The river was full of debris and we kept picking it up in the drogues.

The Catalina has a very slow rate of roll so at air displays we just fly by and turn, showing the aircraft and its retractable wing tip floats and undercarriage. It is a much modified amphibious model with bigger engines than the original pure flying boats which were supplied to the allies in substantial numbers, including RAF Coastal Command for convoy protection duties. It has unique hull blisters and two cupolas at the rear of the hull which protrude from each side and are fantastic for observation as you can actually see all the way along the side of the aircraft – very important in the maritime role."

Capt Keith Sissons, display pilot

The North American B-25 Mitchell was an extremely versatile medium bomber and served in nearly all theatres during WW 2. In the Pacific it excelled as a low level strafer of shipping.

"Whenever I visit the Imperial War Museum at Duxford and gaze at the Fighter Collection's B-25D Mitchell bomber it brings back wartime nostalgia. I was on shore leave in Durban en route to Rangoon when Lt Col Jimmy Doolittle took off from the carrier USS *Hornet* (even though the Mitchell was designed as a land-based attack-bomber!) to lead a squadron of B-52s on the famous Tokyo raid in April 1942. It was the first successful bombing mission over Tokyo by the USAF and we all hoped it would shorten the war in the Far East. It certainly proved the aircraft's performance and ability.

As we have the same first name I've always remembered that the aircraft was named in honour of General 'Billy' Mitchell, pioneer of US military aviation. All the Mitchell bombers I came across in the Far East were flown by the USAF but, with over 9,000 produced, they were in fact operated by eleven air forces during WW 2. Five RAF squadrons were equipped with 800 aircraft which saw service as light, close-support day bombers with the allied armies over Europe.

For the RAF pilots it was often a first time conversion to a tricycle undercarriage and they approached it with terror. But as soon as they started taxiing they were able to appreciate the wonderful all round vision. It was not a complicated aircraft to fly once they were accustomed to the mass of new instruments, knobs and levers. In fact, one pilot once confided in me that it was the first aircraft that he had flown where he actually felt in command!"

Bill White, RAF retired

B-25 MITCHELL

"**M**ost of the Lancaster's fans come just to see the aircraft and don't expect intricate aerobatics. We treat her with so much care and forethought to preserve the airframe. So we have a little display routine of runs and steep turns with the bomb bays open and closed and a G limit of 1.89 to conserve fatigue life. The flypast with the Spitfire and Hurricane is at an economical 150kts and the display routine varies from 110 to 200kts.

Learning to fly the Lancaster was an amazing experience for me, with its big Merlin piston engines and very interesting tail wheel technique, after being trained on jets. I did 13 hours in the Shackleton before I was let loose on the Lancaster. I found her easier to fly than the Shackleton, though there was the odd bounce on landing.

On my very first flight in the Lancaster as a passenger we had an engine failure due to supercharger drive malfunction. But it was no problem flying on three engines as we normally operate the aircraft on half power to conserve engine life. However, I hope it's my only engine out!

Our aircraft, PA 474, is one of only two surviving flying examples, out of a total of 7,377 Lancasters built (3,349 were lost on wartime operations). In 1975, just before the Battle of Britain Memorial Flight moved to RAF Coningsby, PA 474 was adopted by the city of Lincoln, because of the long association between the Lancaster and Bomber Command and the city. She is known as the 'City of Lincoln' and proudly bears the Lincoln coat of arms on the forward fuselage.

In 1963 she was adopted by the RAF Air Historical Branch, destined for the RAF Museum at Hendon after restoration at Wroughton, where she starred in several films including *The Guns of Navarone* and *Operation Crossbow*. However, two years later No 44 Squadron, which had been the first squadron to fly Lancasters in WW 2, was given permission to restore the aircraft to full flying condition."

Sqn Ldr Andy Tomalin, Officer Commanding Battle of Britain Memorial Flight

LANCASTER

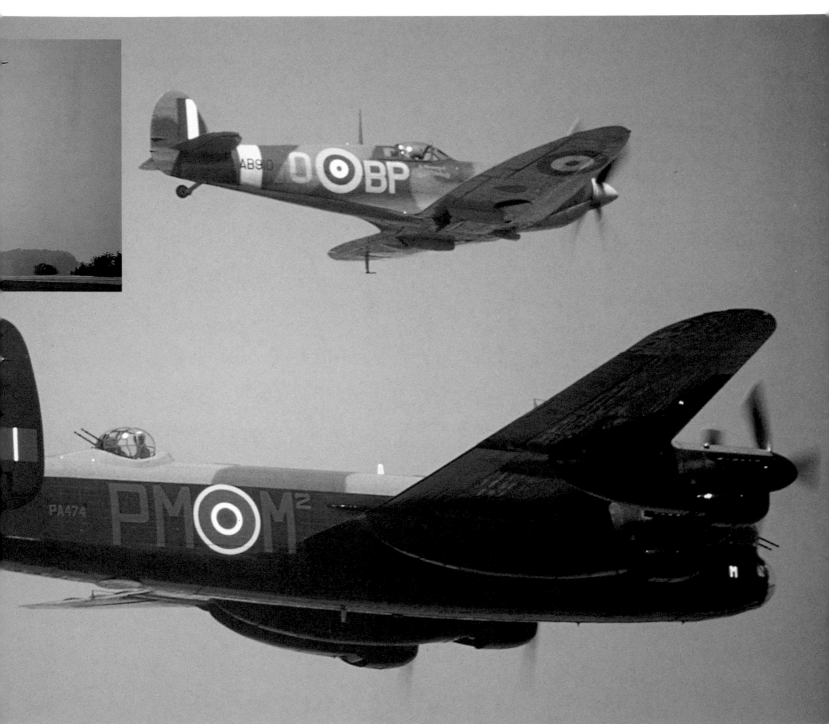

The Avro Lancaster B1 of the Battle of Britain Memorial Flight is one of only two preserved types in the world left flying. The BBMF is a living memorial to the thousands of RAF personnel who served in WW 2.

The Avro Lancaster first flew in January 1941 and was the RAF's main 'heavy' bomber of WW 2. The 'Lanc' or 'big stick' had a crew of 7 and could carry a bomb load of 18,000lbs. She was powered by 4 Rolls Royce Merlins, giving her a top speed of 275mph fully loaded.

Like Grumman's Bearcat (page 63), *the Hawker Sea Fury* was one of the fastest of all propeller driven aircraft. The Sea Fury was a development of the Hawker Tempest and is credited with a number of 'kills' against MiG 15s during the Korean War.

"I flew Hawker Sea Fury N232J across the Atlantic in 1990 from Ohio up to Halifax, Nova Scotia, then to St John's, Newfoundland – to Santa Maria in the Azores and on to Oporto in Portugal – to Southend and finally North Weald where it is hangared. The flight was 18.5 hours duration over two or three months and, cruising at 260kts True Air Speed, we had to choose days when we could pick up the best winds.

Quite the most dangerous part of the trip was the taxi ride from Oporto Airport to our hotel. Because we were in flying suits the crazy driver tried to impress, tearing along at 100mph and screeching up to the traffic lights!

Previously the aircraft had been raced at Reno during 1987-88. Its present owner is Robs Lamplough and he does most of the displays, with a fly past and standard rolling and looping manoeuvres.

It's a magnificent aircraft to fly, very powerful and well harmonised – a real pilot's aircraft. It is, of course, the fastest single piston engined aircraft ever made.

Built in 1947 it served with the Canadian Navy and is painted in Canadian Navy colours. Its first private owner was an American who flew it to the States where it was turned over on its back and then rebuilt with a couple of cannibalised Sea Furies. It's a stock FB11 fighter variant which has been modified to take a passenger by removing the armour plated head rest to make space – a two seater with one set of controls."

Norman Lees, Hawker Sea Fury pilot

SEA FURY

LEFT *The US Navy's carrier-borne Grumman F6F Hellcat* accounted for over 75 per cent of all Japanese aircraft destroyed during WW 2 by the US Navy. The Hellcat first flew in 1942, and was designed as a replacement for its predecessor, the F4F (inset).
BELOW RIGHT *Grumman TBM Avenger.*

"It was a moving moment when US Navy Ace Alex Vraciu was reunited with his Hellcat. It was on 14 July 1991 at the Classic Fighter display, Europe's largest gathering of historic fighter aircraft at Duxford Airfield. The Hellcat was the actual aircraft in which Commander Vraciu scored seven airborne kills in two sorties whilst he and the Hellcat were serving with Navy Fighting-Squadron VF6, and it appears in his US Navy livery. Californian Alex and his wife Kay were our special guests, and at the end of the display F6F-3 40467 Hellcat returned to the sky alone to pay tribute to him.

The aircraft is one of the Fighter Collection's more recent acquisitions. Acquired from Ed Maloney, it arrived during 1990 by sea and was assembled in time to appear at the final Duxford show of that season in Royal Navy markings. However, during March 1991 it was resprayed in its original colours and re-registered as G-BTCC. It is the only Hellcat flying outside the US.

The 2,200hp Grumman Hellcat was undoubtedly one of the most successful fighter aircraft of all time. Supremacy over the Japanese in the air was made possible to a large degree by its arrival. This remarkably tough and manoeuvrable fighter was credited with some 5,000 enemy aircraft destroyed. It was a real all rounder, effective at any altitude.

The Hellcat also operated in Europe with the British Fleet Air Arm as well as with the United States Navy and Marine Corps."

The Fighter Collection team

F6F HELLCAT

The Grumman F8F Bearcat was the ultimate piston engined fighter of the US Navy. Its incredible climb rate was actually better than that of most contemporary jets. These images show the Fighter Collection's F8F Bearcat; this machine is owned and flown by Stephen Grey.

"Our F8F Grumman Bearcat is one of our longer residents. It became part of the Fighter Collection at Duxford in 1984, having been flown from the States across the Atlantic by ferry pilot John Crocker in 1981. He must have been listening to every beat of the engine! It was then based in Switzerland and appeared at an airshow at Anemasse soon after arrival. After joining the Fighter Collection it soon became part of the UK airshow circuit. It carries to this day its original colours of the famous 'Red Rippers' US Navy Squadron VF-41, one of the first squadrons to operate the aircraft in late 1945.

It was one of the fastest piston engined aircraft to be built. It's smaller and lighter than the Hellcat and gives a spectacular and agile display. It was originally intended for the US Navy, to combat the Japanese Kamikaze suicide attacks on naval shipping during the latter part of WW 2. But it never saw service, for the war ended. However, it was used as a ground attack aircraft by the French Air Force in French Indo-China."

Peter Rushen, chief engineer, The Fighter Collection

F8F BEARCAT

CHAPTER 3

FAST & FURIOUS

If you have never visited an airshow, then you should go to one if only for the experience of the sounds – every machine has its own audible signature. Some aircraft purr, some throb and some bleat. The aircraft in this chapter are the fast jets and their audible signatures need to be heard to be believed.

Their distinctive sound is that of air being sucked in one end and spat out the other, much like the sound of thunder about 100 feet above your head. These sleek and incredible machines are captivating and awe-inspiring, and as they rocket through the air just above your head the sound takes your breath away. You have to be there to feel it – there is no other sensation like it.

A Tornado with its wings fully back, and coming towards you at close to the speed of sound, is a stunning visual experience, then as it passes you (if you can follow it!) the sound hits you. It is like a wall of noise that affects you physically and nearly knocks you over. As the Tornado executes a vertical climb with afterburner glowing, followed by the sound of air being torn apart, you are left stunned and fumbling for the programme to see what's next, hoping that it will be another jet.

'Fast & Furious' shows many of today's front line aircraft that regularly attend the airshow meets around the world.

Panavia Tornado GR-1

ABOVE *A MiG-29 pilot of the Czech and Slovakian Airforce* 'getting familiar' with an F-15 Eagle *during the International Air Tattoo at Fairford. With the radical changes taking place in Eastern Europe, scenes such as this will be seen more and more at Western airshows and multi-national events.*

Although the F-15 is twenty years old it is still right amongst the leaders in the air combat league. Its combat capability has been demonstrated on many occasions by the Israeli Air Force, whose pilots have nothing but praise for their aircraft, and most recently during the Gulf War when F-15s of the USAF and RSAF (Royal Saudi Air Force) flew offensive and defensive missions. The F-15 came out as the top-scoring fighter with at least 36 confirmed kills. This was also the operational debut of the two-seat F-15E Strike Eagle.

There can be no better fighter than the Eagle. It packs a big punch of missiles and guns, goes a long way, and out-flies anything it meets. The aircraft feels right as soon as you strap in: everything is readily to hand, not like the ergonomic mess of so many other combat aircraft. 'Bitching Betty' (the aircraft's talking warner) takes a bit of getting used to but you'll soon learn to take notice of what she says. The weapons system is fantastic and the radar makes locking up to targets so easy – point and shoot!

Sure, there are other aircraft that fly as well – almost – as the Eagle, but none of them have the all-round missile capability we have. I would put my aircraft up against the others any day."

F-15 Squadron Commander, Bitburg, Germany , USAFE

During an altitude test in 1975 an F-15 Eagle fired up its engines while stationary on the runway, then rocketed up to 40,000ft in less than one minute. By the time the Eagle had stopped climbing, she was over 103,000ft above the earth.

F-15 EAGLE

ABOVE *This French Dassault Super Etendard 1NM,* from the 17F Landivisiau of the French navy, is a potent shipboard and landbased strike fighter. This very agile jet is capable of carrying the Exocet anti-ship missile, which was used by the Argentine forces during the Falklands Conflict to devastating effect.

LEFT *The Super Etendard trailing wing-tip vortices.* This dramatic effect is a combination of high speed and low pressure and happens when the atmosphere is moist.

SUPER ETENDARD

The Soviet Union's latest fighter, the Sukhoi SU-27, *code-named 'Flanker', is a stunning example of Soviet fighter technology. It is one of the world's most potent combat aircraft, with an advanced fly-by-wire control system, and is a first for the Soviet aircraft industry.*

"They call them 'Russkiye Veetyaze' – the 'Russian Knights'. They're the newest and latest Soviet display team, formed in 1991. In Russian folklore a young warrior renowned for his strength and his ability to defend his motherland was called a 'Veetyaz', roughly the equivalent of the old English Knight.

The six SU-27 'Flanker' aircraft in the team include four single-seat and two twin-seat aircraft. With a top speed of Mach 1 at low level and Mach 2 at high level the display demonstrates to the maximum the high manoeuvring power and capability of an exceptional combat aircraft. The Flanker is powered by two Lylulka AL-31 turbofans.

The team is based at Moscow Kubinka airfield, part of the Moscow Military District, and is fully operational. The team leader is Lieutenant Colonel Vladimir Petrovitch Bazhenov, a 'pilot first class' and squadron commander at Kubinka.

The team made their UK public debut on 21 September 1991 at RAF Finningley and RAF Leuchars at the station airshows. However, the SU-27 Flanker first appeared in the UK at the 1990 Farnborough Show and proved to be a real crowd-pleaser."

Flt Lt Ken Delve, defence analyst

SU-27 'FLANKER'

MiG-29 'FULCRUM'

"They're calling it NATO's finest close-in dog-fighter, made in Russia. Inherited along with huge quantities of Soviet military equipment in the unification of the two Germanys, the Mikoyan MiG-29 was soon evaluated as the most capable light fighter, outclassing NATO's F-4 Interceptors.

When it 'joined' the Luftwaffe and was flown by Western pilots who were trained on type, searching trials against some current Western types included mock dog-fights in which the MiG-29 won every time. Its sturdy structure withstands huge centrifugal (g) forces. Whereas the best Western fighters can withstand 9g, the MiG was found to have an absolute limit of 14g and can fly at much greater angles of attack.

No mere airshow gimmick, its 'flipup' facility of 30^0 for quick manoeuvre in forward flight is for sustained periods, and as much as a phenomenal 80^0 can be briefly reached allowing the pilot to point his 'sights' at an enemy aircraft below or above his direction of flight. It's a deadly combination in combat flight allowing the MiG-29 missile to fly off at any angle.

Though equipped with sophisticated radar and infra-red systems, coalition pilots in the Gulf War who had already evaluated the aircraft found that Soviet suppliers had not included the latest missiles and radar in the Iraqi MiG-29s."

Coalition pilot, Kuwait 1991

The Soviet Union's MiG (Mikoyan Gurevich) 29, code-named 'Fulcrum' by NATO, is an air superiority fighter that is on a par with similar Western fighters. This machine has the ability to stand on its tail from a horizontal flying position and fly belly first in what is now termed the 'Cobra' manoeuvre.

"A high speed run at about 730 mph before a final upward zoom – that's when you get the vaporisation – a big fan shape coming off the canopy and round the middle of the Lightning. It's a match of high speed and low pressure and happens when the atmosphere is moist.

As you approach the speed of sound (about .95 Mach) you start developing shockwaves and you get 'shimmer' off the humped canopy, with the semi-circle of condensation just behind the main shockwave, occurring halfway down the aircraft.

When the English Electric Lightning first joined the squadrons it was the fastest interceptor of its day. In the early days there were no two-seat Lightnings and your first flight was by yourself (after about ten hours in the simulator). The instructor flew in formation with you.

After about three years a two-seat trainer was introduced. Everyone wanted to fly supersonic in it. We carried a lot of passengers and formed a '1,000 Miles an Hour Club'. Then Concorde came along and stole our thunder.

The Lightning F Mk 3 in the Strike Command Lightning display was a delightful aircraft to roll and slow roll. Its high performance would take it a long way from the display area so the aim was a series of manoeuvres which would demonstrate its performance without taking it too far away. These included a flat 360° turn at full power, about 500mph, a steep wing over at 200mph, a dive for a loop, entered at 450mph, and an inverted run."

Peter Clee, former Strike Command Lightning display pilot

The classic shape of the English Electric Lightning interceptor. *This unusual design had the engines stacked one on top of the other. The Lightning was the first single seat RAF fighter to exceed the speed of sound in level flight and it went on to reach speeds of 1,500mph. The Lightning gave over 20 years' service before being retired in the 1980s.*

LIGHTNING

F-16 FIGHTING FALCON

"It is without doubt the fighter pilot's dream machine – you can see out of it, and how. It turns like nothing else around, and accelerates like a thoroughbred. I almost feel sorry for the other guy! The F-16 can truly be called the warplane of the free world, taking over that name from the F-5 Freedom Fighter; developed as a lightweight and relatively cheap fighter, the F-16 entered service with the USAF in 1979. Since then the type has become multi-role and a best-seller worldwide; orders stand at 3,000 plus, with every sign of going much higher. F-16 units played an important role in the Gulf War, taking full advantage of their multi-role capability to undertake a wide range of tasks.

The cockpit feels strange at first with the reclined seat and the lack of a central 'stick'. The side-stick is just like a computer game, but after a while it seems quite natural. One trip and you are a convinced F-16 driver – plug in the burners and sit the thing on its tail and off you go! The ability to pull 9g in combat is fantastic; it's easy to get out of trouble and even easier to cut down the opposition's choices and get into a firing position."

F-16A pilot, Royal Netherlands Air Force (Koninklijke Luchtmacht), 323 Sqn Leeuwarden

The Fighting Falcon is fast becoming one of the Western world's most sought-after aircraft *due to its superb performance, handling characteristics, cost, and minimal maintenance times. The F-16 is currently serving with Bahrain, Belgium, Denmark, Egypt, Greece, Indonesia, Israel, Netherlands, Norway, Pakistan, Singapore, South Korea, Thailand, Turkey, and the United States.*

RIGHT *A General Dynamics F-16A Fighting Falcon of the Royal Netherlands Air Force in a 60° climb-out, with a full afterburner and smokewinders to match. The F-16, like the Mirage, is one of the few aircraft on today's airshow circuit to use smokewinders. These can give a high degree of visibility to a manoeuvrable machine like the F-16.*
FOLLOWING PAGES *A Belgian F-16 returns to the hard stand after a successful display.*

RAF Panavia Tornado GR-1s based at the Al Muharraq air base in Bahrain. These machines are still wearing their 'desert pink' colour scheme, although somewhat faded and flaking after months in a harsh environment during and after Operation Desert Storm.

The Panavia Tornado Interdictor / Strike variant (IDS) of the German Navy. The Tornado has become one of the best interdictor aircraft ever designed. Similar in function to the F-111, the Tornado proved itself during the recent Gulf Conflict. In its RAF role it is called the GR-1.

The Tornado GR-1 entered operational service ten years ago and since then it has become the most significant non-American warplane in the NATO inventory, serving with the RAF, Luftwaffe, Marineflieger, and AMI. In 1991 RAF and Royal Saudi Air Force (RSAF) Tornados played a key role in the United Nations action against Iraq, undertaking deep penetration missions to attack vital targets such as airfields and command installations. The main advantage that the Tornado gave to the Allied air forces of Operation Desert Storm was its ability to locate and hit pinpoint targets day or night and in any weather.

The most amazing aspect of the Tornado is the superb accuracy and reliability of the nav-attack system. The heart of the computer-based system is controlled from the back seat by the navigator, presenting mission data to the TV/TABS (visual display screens) and to the pilot's HUD (head-up display). This, combined with a very high resolution radar, means that the crew can carry out blind attacks on even the smallest of targets.

Add to this the aircraft's excellent 'hands-off' Terrain-Following Radar (TFR), which follows the contours of the ground, even at high speed, and you have a truly remarkable combat aircraft. The Tornado is also no slouch: when it comes to air combat with two Sidewinder missiles, plus two 27mm cannon, the aircraft is well able to look after itself in a fight!

One of the biggest threats to our low level style of operations comes from ground-based missiles and guns. The extensive electronic warfare suite, managed from the back seat, provides a full range of active and passive counter-measures – essential in the hostile air environment of the modern battlefield."

Tornado GR-1 pilot, Bahrain 1991

TORNADO

TORNADO

Designed as a long-range interceptor, the Air Defence Version (ADV) of the Tornado entered service with the RAF in November 1984. Like its 'mud-moving' variant it saw operational service during the Gulf War; although never called upon to engage the Iraqi Air Force, the F-3s flew hundreds of Combat Air Patrol (CAP) sorties along the Saudi border.

As an interceptor the F-3 is superb. The aircraft system, based upon the Foxhunter radar, displays tactical information in a readily usable format, and can be tied into data provided by other agencies to provide a full picture of the air scenario. The four Skyflash missiles give a long-range killing capability, whilst the four Sidewinders are vital for any close combat work, and if it really comes down to it then the 27mm cannon may provide a vital edge. One very important factor is that it is a very comfortable aircraft, no small consideration when long CAPs have to be flown with air-to-air refuelling so that we can stay on station for many hours.

From the pilot's point of view it's a good aircraft to fly, with plenty of power and responsive on the controls – it even turns well in most configurations. The aim of the combat game is to get the first shot away before the other guy can, and working as a team in the Tornado makes all the difference."

Tornado F-3 pilot, Royal Saudi Air Force

Also available in light grey, in this case the Tornado Air Defence Variant (ADV). *This version is longer than its IDS counterpart and is designed as a long range all weather air defence fighter. As such, it is in service with the RAF and Royal Saudi Air Force.*

"In performance and weapon-carrying the AV-8B almost doubled the capability of its predecessor. Our US Marine Corps AV-8Bs saw action in the Gulf War, achieving one of the highest sortie rates of any type in theatre.

There are so many superlative aspects to the Harrier it is hard to know what to talk about. I suppose the most obvious factor is the ability to operate away from complex airfields – the problems of being tied to an airfield Main Operating Base (MOB) were aptly demonstrated during the Gulf War when the Iraqi Air Force was virtually grounded because of attacks on its airfields. All we have to do is go find a large clump of trees, a sand dune, or anything else to hide behind. It's very hard to find a dispersed Harrier base unless you know where it is. Some of the pilots think that the hardest part of a mission is trying to find the right patch of ground again! Once on the ground it takes no more than a few minutes for the aircraft to vanish out of sight into its 'hide', then the groundcrew can get down to re-arming and re-fuelling – not many minutes later and the aircraft is ready to go again.

The capability of the Harrier has been upgraded again with the entry into service of the GR-7 'Night Attack' variant, equipped with sensors which allow for night and limited bad weather operations."

AV-8B Harrier 11 pilot, US Marine Corps

HARRIER

The BAe Harrier GR-5 *was designed as a replacement for the Harrier GR-3. Manufactured jointly by McDonnell Douglas (as the AV-8B) and British Aerospace (GR-5), the Harrier has proved to be a superb fighting machine.*

__The revolutionary General Dynamics F-111__ was the world's first genuine all weather interdictor; coupled with its ability to vary its wings and terrain following radar (TFR), this machine is very fast and sneaky. A product of the 1960s, the F-111 is in service with two air forces, the USAF and Royal Australian Air Force (F-111C). Depicted here are F-111 Es of the 20th TFW (Tactical Fighter Wing).

The Gulf War was yet another conflict which added to the laurels of the F-111 story; since its introduction in 1969 the type has seen operational service in Vietnam and in the spectacular raid on Libya in April 1986. Designed as a strategic bomber the F-111 suffered a number of problems in its early years, although these were soon overcome, and the type went on through numerous upgrades, and threats of being replaced, to achieve an admirable reputation.

One of the great advantages of sitting side-by-side is that I can glance over and see what the WSO (Weapons Systems Officer) is doing; the same goes for him – especially if we are heading into dirty weather and the TFR is engaged. It's a great confidence boost. Sure we lose out a bit on lookout, but our aim is to stay away from trouble in the first place, and the aircraft's systems allow us to fly in weather that few other people would even look at. Supersonic at low level is no problem – the ride is so smooth that you can only tell the speed by looking at the needle. One of our biggest problems at low level is birds – but the engines have proved themselves to be pretty good at chewing them up and spitting them out with barely a cough. The F-111 was never officially given any name like the Phantom etc, so we called it the Aardvark, because its long nose is shaped like that of an anteater. I think that most of us now call it either the 'Vark' or the 'Lizard'."

F-111E pilot, 20th TFW Upper Heyford

The EF-111A Raven is a reworked version of the F-111A. *Grumman Aerospace produced 42 examples of this machine, and it is one of the West's most sophisticated Electronic Countermeasures platforms. These examples are from the USAF 42nd ECS based at Upper Heyford in Oxfordshire.*

Like the F-111 (previous page) the EF-111 was never given an official name. Most EF-111 'drivers' call their mounts the Raven. Other names in use are the the 'Electric Fox' and 'Spark Vark'.

EF-111A RAVEN

The McDonnell Douglas F/A-18 Hornet *excels as a fighter as well as a very efficient strike platform. The unusual wing of the Hornet has very large leading edge extensions (LEXs) which protrude all the way forward to the cockpit area. The idea of the LEX is that very strong air flow vortices are forced over the wing, giving the pilot the ability to maintain control even at extreme angles of attack and giving added lift to the wing in general.*

ABOVE **This aircraft, an EF-18** from Ala 15 of the Spanish Air Force, returns from a display in its 'carrier' mode.

"Because of the fantastic, explosive acceleration of the Hornet during a high G turn, pilots often suffer from loss of consciousness. This machine can build up Gs so fast that the pilots are not prepared for it. This aircraft is just the hottest thing around in terms of high technology. Everything I need to see is in front of me within the head-up display (HUD), so I can really concentrate on what I have to do without having to move in my seat to find some system or other. It really becomes part of you the moment you strap this potent machine on. It is the most exhilarating experience I have ever had. It's something I dreamed about as a kid. You don't have much time to sit back and enjoy your time as things happen real fast, though I will make damn sure that I make the most of this experience."

F/A-18 pilot, Royal Australian Air Force

F/A-18 HORNET

The classic lines of the Dassault Mirage 111 which first took to the air in November 1956. Dassault have continually improved this basic design and externally there is little difference between the marques. This example is with the Belgian Air Force.

ABOVE *First flown in December 1966,* the Dassault Mirage F1 is a high wing breakaway from the standard Mirage Delta design concept. This example is with the Spanish Air Force.
RIGHT *Dassault's latest marque of the classic European design,* the Mirage 2000C of the French Air Force, seen here performing at Farnborough complete with smokewinders.

One of the mainstay types of the French Air Force, the Mirage 2000 entered service in 1983 and now operates in a variety of roles. In common with its Mirage 111 predecessor, it has proved to be an export success, especially in the Middle East. Although it maintains the single-engine and delta-wing configuration so reminiscent of Dassault designs, the Mirage 2000 is very much a third-generation agility combat aircraft in respect of its flying control systems and avionics.

The Mirage was a worthy winner of the International Air Tattoo best solo display award for 1991, after the pilot showed his aircraft to its full potential with a classic combination of slow speed and high speed manoeuvres. Some of the 'square corners' were astounding, and the low speed high-alpha pass demonstrated the supreme controllability of the Mirage. This was voted by the NATO pilot group opinion!

After the somewhat 'heavy' Mirage 111, the agility of the 2000 is like a breath of fresh air. The aircraft is very light on the controls, requiring only small control inputs to achieve the required manoeuvre. Even with a full load of missiles there is little change to the flight envelope."

Mirage 2000 pilot, Escuadron de Chasse 5/330, French Air Force

MIRAGE

Refracted polarised evening light *seen in the canopy of an A-7D Corsair of the USAF, Pittsburgh Air National Guard.*

Flying in the colours of the Força Aérea Portuguesa, these Ling-Temco-Vought (LTV) A-7 Corsairs are the standard attack aircraft of the FAP.

"**W**hen we took the A-7E into Vietnam in 1970 we had an airplane of unsurpassed excellence – it had the best weapons delivery system yet devised, very accurate *and* reliable, plus a 20mm Vulcan cannon to go with the selection of bombs and missiles. The pilots had every confidence in the ability of the A-7 to bring them back in one piece: it was such a strong chunk of metal that it seemed almost to shrug off the ground fire. The damage a single flight of aircraft could inflict was enormous – as many a VC target in Nam discovered. It's a shame that the aircraft has not received the write-up it deserves.

Designed as a ship-based strike/attack aircraft, although with multi-role capability built in, the A-7 entered service in 1966 and saw operational service in Vietnam. Early problems with losses due to ingestion of steam from the catapult launch took some while to correct, but overall the A-7 was shaping up well as a sturdy and reliable jet capable of lifting a large weapon load.

The Portuguese Air Force still operates the A-7, and from time to time sends aircraft to appear on the UK airshow circuit. Unfortunately, the aircraft never appear in the flying display, but they are welcome rare additions to the static park."

US Marine Corps A-7 pilot, USS *Kittyhawk*

"**O**ne of the things that I particularly enjoyed about Red Flag was the flying. Weather permitting, and it usually was, you flew once a day and once you got on to the range areas it could get to be fairly robust, because there are all sorts of threat simulation devices out there. Mission control radars – stuff like that – and a thing called 'Smoky Sam' that they can actually fire and looks like a real surface-to-air missile. It's harmless, of course, but it still gets your attention. So part of your attention will be focused on avoiding the defences, and part on getting through to your target. This might be an airfield, or a concentration of armoured vehicles, or even a Sam site.

It isn't just ground threats that have to be avoided, though. In addition you know that 'Red Air' – they're the bad guys – will be out there somewhere, and since there are only a limited number of ingress routes, it's fairly easy for them to mount combat air patrols and bounce you as you pass through. In a real war, naturally you'd try to avoid 'hot spots' for fairly obvious reasons. In 'Flag' you can't do that, so somebody almost always gets 'tapped' and then it's a case of trusting that your defensive tactics will be sufficient to beat the threat. Sometimes they are – sometimes they aren't . . .

For us, of course, it's all down to putting bombs on targets and it's always a good feeling when your attack goes well, but the hairy moments aren't over because you still have to egress the area, and 'Red Air' aren't averse to having a go at you on the way out. In the Jaguar, which isn't a dogfighter, the best tactic is to stay low and run like hell, while using your defensive kit – jamming pods, flares and that sort of stuff – to counter the threat. Again, sometimes you succeed, sometimes you don't, but at least you get to walk away and think about it afterwards.

Most of the thinking is done in the post-mission debriefing sessions and that is when the real lessons are learned. They can sometimes go on for hours and the Yanks have got some amazing equipment at Nellis. It's a bit like the ultimate computer game but on the big screen, and they can replay the entire scenario. I'll tell you one thing though, it certainly stops all the arguments you used to get about who killed who."

RAF Jaguar GR-1 pilot, exercise *Red Flag*, Nevada

LEFT **The SEPECAT Jaguar GR-1** is a single seat strike aircraft, the prime role of which is the direct tactical support of ground forces. When the Jaguar is down low it is a very slippery customer as it is not easy to see visually and has a very small radar signature.
BELOW **Jaguar T2,** two-seat trainer variant.

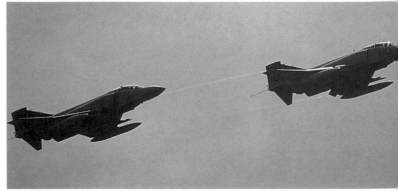

The F-4 Phantom was designed as a carrier-borne aircraft and was one of the most rugged and versatile of all jet military aircraft and the most successful all-round 60s production – 4,000 were completed by 1970.

A true classic, the McDonnell Douglas F-4 Phantom 2. The 'Fabulous Phantom', or 'Big Ugly' has been produced in more numbers than any other supersonic jet fighter, with a total of 5,100 examples built. Japan, in addition, has built under licence a further 156 machines. F-4 production ceased in 1979. These images show an F-4J (UK) of the RAF, purchased from the US Navy in the early 1980s for defence of the Falkland Islands. In US Navy service this machine flew during the Vietnam War from the USS America, as part of VF-74.

"It's an aircraft you wanted to get back into, and when you did it became an extension of you and your observer (navigator if you're RAF). It would look after you and give you plenty if you pushed the edges of the flight envelope. It has only one 'Outside the Envelope' unfriendly side, its flat spin. As the manual made clear, 'There is no known recovery from a flat spin.' Even that statement implied that there might be some unknown recovery action. To fight with the 'Toom' you kept her wound up 420 to 540kts low-level and Mach 1.2 high-level. It's an aircraft of sweeping performance and ability. In the world of aircraft ordnance, if an aircraft could fire it, drop it, or just switch it on, the chances are that at some time or other it had been done from a 'Toom'. In Vietnam the US Phantoms would go in to recce a target; anti SAM 'Wild Weasel' Phantoms would then go in to clear the way for the bomber variant Phantoms flying in protected by the fighter versions. The recce ones then went back on battle damage assessment (BDA) missions. The airframe could do anything, depending on the avionics you put in it. In fencing terms it's a sabre – a quick slashing attacker and if you didn't succeed you went out the other side, re-grouped and came back again. It was definitely not a close quarter dog-fighting machine.

We used to have a clean limit of 8.5g below 0.72M, and 6.5g above 1.05M, but now it's lower. It's an old but loved aircraft now, but when I flew in the Fleet Air Arm in the early 70s the F4Ks were fresh from McDonnell.

The British Phantoms have clean-burning, non-smoking, Rolls Royce Spey engines and the Navy version had improved Mk.203 Speys giving faster reheat responses at low level (handy if you missed the deck landing wires!). It was easy to operate from carriers. The take-off attitude for catapult launches was achieved by a special extending nose gear and glide slope control on landing made effective by use of the throttles. If you closed them you lost most of your lift. Air was bled from the engine compressors to the wings and out aft of the leading edges. This kept the airflow smooth over the wings at low speed/high angles of attack. As a fighting machine it has a two-man crew of pilot and observer, who operated what was then a state-of-the-art Doppler Radar to find your targets.

The manual says a speed of Mach 2.1 is achievable, but in practice this was difficult. The fastest speed I ever got from a clean 'Toom' was Mach 2.0 and a TAS of 1,214kts, and on that occasion I found after I landed that the paint on the leading edges was all blistered with heat.

On one sortie I flew a 'Toom' out of Lee-on-Solent. It had landed with engine trouble and only managed to stop by using the CHAG arrester wire gear there. The normal take-off procedure was to select full reheat on the roll to guarantee take-off. The runways used by Phantoms are normally long enough to abandon take-off if the reheat didn't light up. You weren't going to make it without it! Although the aircraft was 'clean' and as light as possible, with just enough fuel for the flight, the 4,200-odd foot runway 23 was totally inadequate. So we closed the coast road at the end of the runway in case of any mishaps, backed the aircraft wheels to the threshold of 23, tested each engine reheat against chocks on the grass behind the runway threshold, and went for it. They lit up and I climbed to 40,000 feet, never reached the Isle of Wight coast, closed the throttles and 'glided' down to our base at Yeovilton, a flight of just 10 minutes."

Jonathon Whaley, former Fleet Air Arm AW1 pilot, currently film and stunt pilot

F-4 PHANTOM

ABOVE *An F-4F of the German Luftwaffe* tucks in its gear with afterburner ablaze.

LEFT *An F-4G 'Wild Weasel' of the USAFE's 52nd TFW,* based at Spangdahelm in Germany. As a result of bitter lessons learnt in Vietnam and the Middle East, the 'G' version of the venerable Phantom was built as a response to the very accurate SAM. The missile detection and launch system is located under the nose radome. The black missiles on the intake deflector are evidence that the system worked effectively during the recent Gulf Conflict.

F-4 PHANTOM

The futuristic shape of Lockheed's SR-71 Blackbird *first flew almost 20 years ago. Its incredible performance gave it speeds of up to 2,000 mph and its skin temperature heated up to around 320⁰ C over the entire airframe; even the engine nozzles became white hot. The Blackbird's role was as a high altitude reconnaissance machine.*

"**P**reparing for a mission in the SR-71 is like preparing for a trip into space, right down to putting on space-suits. It takes 30 minutes and the help of three other people to get into the kit – but it's worth it when you know that it's designed to save your life should the aircraft develop a problem when you are way up high.

Although now withdrawn from service, the SR-71 continues to hold a fascination for many aviation enthusiasts; the prospect of seeing a Blackbird make an appearance at an air display was enough to make people drive hundreds of miles. Entering service in 1966 this super-secret strategic-reconnaissance aircraft was very much a part of the Cold War, with East and West keeping a very close eye on each other.

For the unwary groundcrew the Blackbird can literally be a 'hot ship'. The aircraft skin gets really hot when the bird is up there flying fast, and it takes some time for it to cool down – so best don't touch it for a while after it lands! The biggest 'no no' is to walk on the surface of the wings without putting down the protective mats. Other than that, she's a good bird to work with."

SR-71 maintenance chief, 9th SRW, Kadena, Okinawa

SR-71 BLACKBIRD

"The A-10 is surely one of the strangest-looking combat aircraft around – but it wasn't designed to win beauty prizes, it was designed with the very specific purpose of killing Warsaw Pact tanks in large numbers. Entering service in March 1977 it brought a great improvement in the NATO anti-tank capability. Thunderbolts were heavily involved in the Gulf War and, along with Apache helicopters, accounted for a great many Iraqi tanks and vehicles.

It may be an ugly mother but it packs a punch like a rhino. The designers certainly took everything into consideration. Attacking the kind of targets we do means that you have to have an airplane that can look after itself – and that includes taking damage. As a pilot I feel very reassured by the armoured 'bath' which surrounds the cockpit area.

Too many aircraft designs ignore the problems of rapid re-arming, but the 'Hog' is different. The gun, despite having over 1,000 rounds of ammunition, is quick and easy to deal with, as are the underwing stations. A good team can have the aircraft ready to go again in a matter of minutes."

A-10 pilot, Saudi Arabia

The Fairchild A-10A is not the world's prettiest aircraft, *with its dubbed name of 'Warthog'. This aircraft is designed to bust tanks with its awesome Avenger 7-barrelled rotary 30mm cannon. The A-10 Thunderbolt 11, as it is officially designated, is one of the West's most potent tank and helicopter airborne attack systems. The A-10 Thunderbolt is capable of operating from freeways and autobahns if its base has been destroyed by attack, and it can shelter under bridges or flyovers between sorties.*

A-10 THUNDERBOLT

The venerable Blackburn Buccaneer S2B is still one of the world's best maritime defence aircraft, even though it is now over 30 years old. Distinguishing features of the Buccaneer are a rotating-door bomb-bay, and large 'butterfly' air brakes which are an extension of the rear fuselage.

"The Buccaneer was designed to operate at very low level over the sea and for the pilot it was very exhilarating. It felt completely at home at 50 feet and 550kts plus. The ride was smooth but it became very noisy at 550kts.

Handling the 'Bucc', as we called it, at high speed was a great joy but it was somewhat hard work in the circuit with boundary layer control; a system that blew air over the ailerons, flaps, and a tailplane flap to augment lift at slow speed from the rather small wings. A highly manoeuvrable aircraft, its rate of roll was astonishing though you could not pitch and roll hard at the same time. It was a case of pitching and then rolling. Failure to observe this little quirk could result in the fin breaking off.

The airbrakes were wonderful and extending them at 500 kts was dramatic, as they gave the aircraft a higher rate of descent than any other, without building up speed. The opposition couldn't stay with you and were forced to overtake. In Germany a favourite trick was to lure the F104 into a six o'clock position at low level and then extend the butterfly air brakes – the 104 would sail straight through your twelve o'clock, throttling back like mad.

We all have moments of excitement and fear in flying and my time on the Bucc was no exception. We kept the aircraft in pairs in hardened shelters, with the wings folded for convenience. One night I forgot to spread the wings.

Fortunately, I was held on the runway waiting for take-off clearance. Because of the sweep, the wings are a long way behind one's peripheral vision. However, I noticed red flashes and realised with horror that the anti-collision beacon on the fuselage behind the cockpit was reflected off the folded wings. I cursed the navigator for missing the check, spread the wings and took off. . .

The Americans were amazed to see the aircraft being manoeuvred so violently at such extremely low levels on Red Flag exercises. It was one of the few times that the Yanks openly respected the Limeys! It was a highly successful low level bomber – which could have been more effective with modern avionics."

Hugh John, former Buccaneer pilot

BUCCANEER

ABOVE, BELOW & BOTTOM LEFT **Buccaneers were part of the coalition air defences during Operation Desert Storm** in the recent Gulf Conflict. As such they wore the 'desert pink' colour scheme common to all Royal Air Force aircraft that took part.

CHAPTER 4

HEAVY METAL

The types of aircraft portrayed in Heavy Metal are the giants of the skies: the Bombers, the Heavy Lifters, Tankers, Maritime Patrol and Airborne Surveillance. Most of the initial design requirements for these machines meant that they had to stay aloft for anything up to 12 hours at a time, carrying vast quantities of personnel, equipment, weapons, fuel and electronic systems. They were built to be big and their operational roles usually dictated that they would be behind the scenes, working around the clock day and night, and never receiving the same profile as the piston pursuits or fast jets.

With more and more restored types and frontline operating aircraft being seen on the airshow circuits today, we are often stunned by the versatility of machines like the Nimrod or AN-225, for example. Big and fat does not always equate with slow and clumsy, as anyone witnessing a Hercules perform a *Khe Sanh* tactical landing will testify!

Like some of the rare birds of 'Classic Pistons', that only have one or two examples in an airworthy state, 'Heavy Metal' has its rarities, even though they are on the whole a product of the jet age.

There is only one flying example of the Avro Vulcan in the world (and even this may soon be relegated to a static display due to its fatigue life being exceeded). This does not mean that there are no Vulcans available for restoration, though – there are, but they have one major disadvantage over, say, a P-51 restoration project, they are BIG! The amount of time, energy, money and facilities needed are in proportion to the machine's size. A Vulcan is not the easiest aircraft to transport by road, nor is the B-52 an aircraft that could be maintained and operated by a small group of people.

Because of their size, these giants can perform a multiplicity of roles, even ones that were not a part of the initial design specification. This allows some of the 'heavies' of aviation a longevity that enables aircraft like the VC-10 (at left) still to be seen flying operationally 30 or 40 years after their first flight.

The BAC VC-10 K3 air-to-air refuelling tanker. This airframe is a military rebuild of the late 1960s and early '70s Vickers VC-10 airliner.

"There is not much difference in flying the VC-10K and the KC-135 air-to-air refuelling tankers. Basically, the aircraft come up behind you and you wait for it all to happen. It's just the systems that are different. The British use the probe and drogue system whereas we use the solid boom. In the 135 the boom operator works from the rear, lying on his stomach in the body of the aircraft. His calls are followed.

In the RAF the aircraft commander is in charge of the operation while the engineer sits behind the pilots in the cockpit, and operates the fuelling panel. The co-pilot has a camera which shows how things are going along.

There is an old saying, 'There's no rank on the flight deck', and in each system the crew co-ordination is efficient but relaxed. It's a good working environment.

Our missions are similar but we have some extremely lengthy refuelling sorties in the 135. It can be a long time for a guy to lie on his stomach and we've known the boom operator to fall asleep. We've called him and got no reply!

The KC-135 R model is most like the VC-10. Both have powerful engines with great thrust. They're the same vintage and both well maintained.

At first I got confused with 'port' and 'starboard'. We use 'left' and 'right'. You could say I had a language problem!

My first evaluation flight in the 135 was from Wright Patterson Airport in Dayton, Ohio. We were struck by lightning. The instruments went haywire and the engineer jumped up, shouting 'We've been hit,' and promptly knocked himself out on the panel above."

Captain Gary Williams, USAF/RAF exchange pilot/instructor

The KC-135 Stratotanker is one of the prime movers in the US air-to-air refuelling inventory. The 135 is a military re-build of the early civilian Boeing 707 airliner. In its tanking role the 135 can carry 31,200 US gallons of aviation fuel in 21 tanks, 12 in the wings and a further 9 in the fuselage itself. This particular machine, 'Keystone Lady', is a KC-135E and is attached to the Pennsylvania Air National Guard.

KC-135

ABOVE **A thirsty C-130 Hercules** is given a top-up from a Victor K2. This system utilises the probe and drogue technique of the RAF, unlike the solid boom arm of the USAF. RIGHT **Victor crewmen head out** to their mount to refuel Tornado GR-1s during operations in the Gulf.

"The Handley Page Victor Mk 1 was a good old aeroplane that never stopped – but it was made like a brick built s . . . house! We called it the 'ground hog' for we were never sure if it would get off the ground. It needed an awful lot of runway – and we used to call its Bristol Siddeley Sapphire engines 'agricultural'.

At static displays people would come up and ask whether it would go underwater – because of its Jules Verne submarine look.

It entered RAF service in 1958 as a bomber and was converted to the tanker role in 1965, taking over from the Valiant, one of the earliest of the V-bombers.

A colleague of mine took off from RAF Marham straight into an enormous flock of seagulls. All four engines were ingested but he managed to fly the circuit and land safely. There were sixty birds dead on the runway and all the engines had to be changed.

The Mk 2 was a much more advanced aircraft with powerful Conway engines, different electronics and instrumentation. I flew both, air-to-air refuelling all the fighters – Lightnings, Jaguars, F4s, Tornados and Buccaneers. Every trip was different and I enjoyed them all."

Dave Parker, former Victor pilot

The Handley Page Victor K2 is nearing the end of its long operational life. The Victor started life as one of Britain's fleet of three V-bombers (Victor, Vulcan and Valiant), and it is now used as an air-to-air refuelling tanker.

OVERLEAF *A Victor K2 trails its drogue* while the receiver ship, in this case a C-130 Hercules, slides into position.

VICTOR

Lockheed's superlative C-130 Hercules first flew in 1954 and is still being produced. The 'Herky Bird' or 'Fat Albert' is in service with nearly every air force of the western world. It has performed practically every conceivable role, from fire fighting to gunship, from transport to tanker, and it just keeps going on and on. The images on these pages show 'Fat Albert' in RAF service, based at RAF Lyneham.

HERCULES

"The Captain turns and smiles and indicates that I should hold on to something solid. Suddenly the horizon rises rapidly outside the cockpit window and vanishes, the nose of the huge Hercules drops like a brick and we are diving at the ground, accelerating to 300mph – my body becomes almost weightless and I prepare for the landing flare. The C-130 dives from about 2,000ft in a near vertical descent. The aircraft needs to create a cushion of air for landing, so as the speed builds up, the vast machine rapidly changes to a horizontal position a few hundred feet from the ground. My knees buckle as the G forces start to act, forcing me to the floor of the cockpit. Within seconds we land and the Captain is applying full reverse pitch on the 13ft diameter propellers, which stops this massive machine in about 4 seconds!

The *Khe Sanh* tactical landing was perfected in Vietnam, due to the hostile small arms fire the crews received on finals. Because the Herc's favoured landing approach was to come in low and fast, they were sitting ducks to anyone with weapons near the approach to Khe Sanh Airbase. The new approach kept the aircraft out of range of small arms, and then dive, flare and land at the last possible moment.

A very spectacular and exhilarating experience. In taking the image opposite, I was very aware of what my partner (in the glass bubble) was experiencing. Afterwards he looked a little pale!"

Jon Davison, photographer & author

As part of the ongoing training programme at RAF Lyneham, crews are instructed in the art of 'tanking' (above), and low-level flying (opposite). C-130 tankers were developed primarily during the long hauls of the Falklands campaign. Like their Victor K2 counterparts they use the probe and drogue system. C-130s in USAF service use the same system, but with two additional drogues, one from each wing tank.

HERCULES

"**W**hen you get a large stream of, say, fifteen Alberts, and very still air, as the aircraft line up over the drop zone you get an awful lot of turbulence created by the aircraft in front of you. This can have quite violent effects on the following aircraft, when you hit someone's backwash suddenly, and because you are dropping troops you are at a very slow speed anyway, so you can get some nasty situations. I've seen an Albert hit a backwash and suddenly go into a 45° bank while he was dropping his troops.

Say you are number seven of the Para stream and you are dropping, then it really can be quite frightening; the aircraft just does its own thing, and because of the slow speed and the reduced control effectiveness it's quite fierce.

I've hit some turbulence when we were dropping a 'wedge' out the back – that's a 2,500lb load of arms and ammunition that goes out prior to the troops' deployment. We hit this backwash and the wedge went out of the aircraft sideways – the turbulence was that great, we dropped a wing and out went the wedge at 45°. If you had three C-130s 4,000 feet away in front of you in formation, each with four 13ft-diameter propeller circles of power pushing the aircraft forward, you can imagine the buffeting you'd be likely to get.

Our aim is to get into the DZ at low level so as not to be detected and get out as quickly as possible, normally at 250ft above the ground, though if we were running or being chased we could go lower, and that can be either over flat ground or valleys."

Captain Max Burton, C-130 pilot

"My most exciting flight in an Air Atlantique Dakota was the first time I sprayed an oil slick in the mouth of the Mersey. At spray height I was aware of the Liver Birds above us, the docks beside us and the ferry in the estuary below, wondering if it was going to sail in front or behind us.

The estuary, one of the worst areas for oil spills, was not wide enough to operate into wind and so we had to spray crosswind. We fly round the basin at about 300ft and spray from 25ft. Spraying is the most amazing fun, getting the Dak down to that height over the sea. The adrenalin flows!

The Dak loves going a long way and settles into an even drone. But you have to show it who's boss. It would play up anyone timid and has a mind of its own, and it's easy to do something totally unexpected, like when you think you're going to do a greaser. It stalls like no tomorrow, dropping a wing at first very sedately, but keeps going down. It's heavy in the turn but quite light in pitch and has a light aircraft mentality, changing handling characteristics with the load.

The company has seven Daks retained by the Ministry of Transport on permanent standby for marine pollution control (the only company in Europe that operates in this way) and three others, one with a very smart passenger kit, another used mainly for freight and a third awaiting restoration.

On the reunification of Germany the company was asked if we had a Dak which took part in the Berlin Airlift. We had, and it was invited to join the celebration fly-past along the Berlin Corridor with an RAF navigator. The crew were treated like royalty, and the aircraft proudly wears to this day a Berlin bear badge presented to it."

Capt Kathy Burnham, Air Atlantique training captain

DC-3 DAKOTA

As venerable as the Hercules on the preceding pages but older! The Douglas DC-3 Dakota, or C-47/R4D, first flew in the 1930s and has become the most successful transport aircraft ever. The 'Dak', like the Hercules, has had many incarnations including floats, internal cannons, skis and many more.

"I had never been to Farnborough before, let alone an airshow, and had never even seen a Russian aeroplane. My husband was with the people on the trade stands, and so I went for a walk amongst the planes.

I remember walking around this huge white thing and thinking, 'This can't fly, it's impossible – they must have towed it here or something.' After a while we were all marshalled back to the spectator enclosures so that the flying programme could start.

I was transfixed by this plane and I kept looking at it all day, it was such an odd shape, but very friendly looking. After watching the fast jets and the little civilian 'puddle jumpers' (so I was told) this Antonov started to move up the runway towards me. The ground trembled as it went past, then this great white whale of a thing just leapt into the air, literally! It just seemed to say to itself 'about here will do' and the thing just jumped up into the sky. I was amazed! As if that wasn't enough, it did a turn and went back the way it came from just above the trees on the other side of the runway, which only seemed a couple of hundred yards away. I couldn't believe it, I think I may be in love with it."

Sally Walsh, first time airshow spectator

The Antonov AN-225 'Dream' is without doubt the world's largest aircraft and has a maximum take-off weight of 600 tons. This Russian monster is designated 'a universal transport system'.

AN-225

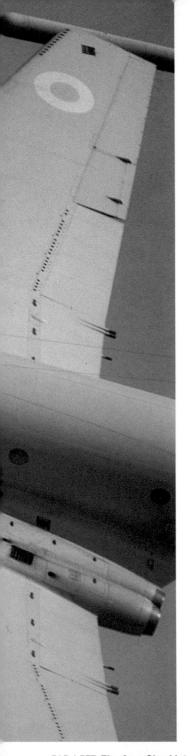

"It's a large and noisy aeroplane! That's the Nimrod's appeal to the crowd, together with its 'double bubble' effect holding an unpressurised pannier underneath the fuselage. The display sequence starts with a run in at 250kts parallel to the crowd, then a steep 360° flaps turn, flashing its searchlight and with bomb doors open. After the next run in, a flaps and gear down turn is followed by two further flaps turns each at 45° away from the crowd and then, cleaned up, a steep climb facing away from the crowd, so that they can see the top of the aircraft. This is followed by a steep descending turn and then a low-and-slow all gear and flaps extended run in past the crowdline. Finally, a fast run in is followed by a very steep climb before it disappears.

After spending the summer of 1983 as display pilot, on 12 November I landed the first Nimrod on the runway at Port Stanley, which had been temporarily repaired with aluminium matting. On 18 November we flew the first non-stop flight home from the Falklands, refuelling in the air three times from Hercules, Victor and Vulcan tankers, a proving flight before the subsequent non-stop flight with Michael Heseltine, then Minister of Defence, on board. Both the MR-1 and then the MR-2 operated out of Ascension Island during the conflict, flying patrols in the South Atlantic.

The Nimrod is the world's only pure jet Maritime Reconnaissance aircraft and is equipped for anti-submarine warfare, surface surveillance, search and rescue and support for naval forces. Derived from the Comet, with the addition of the unpressurised pannier and 12,100 lbs thrust Spey Mk 250 turbofans it was a great improvement on the Shackleton. To further extend loiter time on patrol we can shut down one or both of the outboard engines. A flight duration of nine hours will allow six hours on patrol at 1,000 miles from base.

The MR-2, an upgrade which began in 1981, carried a central computer which allowed the use of more advanced sonobuoys and processed the information much more quickly. It was also fitted with searchwater radar which could detect large or small contacts and compute track and speed. It's still one of the best.

MR-2s were on front line in the Gulf, where, based at Seeb, they were involved in surveillance. Three Nimrod R1s operated by No 51 Squadron, which calibrate radio and radar, were based in support at RAF Akrotiri."

Wg Cdr Mike Blee, Officer Commanding No 51 Squadron

FAR LEFT *The Avro Shackleton* maritime reconnaissance aircraft.
LEFT *The De Havilland Comet* civilian airliner of the 1960s.
ABOVE & RIGHT *The Hawker Siddeley Nimrod MR-2* maritime reconnaissance aircraft .

NIMROD

The unmistakable lines of the British Avro Vulcan. *The Vulcan first flew in August 1952 and was designed to use the Blue Steel nuclear Stand-off bomb, and it was also capable of carrying 21,000lbs of conventional bombs.*

"We all had the greatest admiration for the Vulcan – a wonderful aircraft for its weight and size. With its spectacular delta wing it was very different to fly. You used a lot of rudder, in fact at circuit height we almost flew it with our feet. Its fighter controls were very precise and the control column moved very easily. Originally designed for one pilot, you had to know how to get in and out of the cockpit! The 80,000lbs thrust from its four improved Olympus turbojets was 50 per cent more than needed. This was because it was built to carry the weight of the Skybolt missile which was cancelled.

For the Falklands episode we had to learn about air-to-air refuelling – a one week course of five flights, whereas normally the course of twenty trips lasted six to nine months. So we took a Victor tanker pilot who flew down in the right hand seat and was replaced by the co-pilot when we reached our destination. I remember our Victor pilot well. He was an old timer and when the action started he just went to sleep in the back. On the return journey we listened to the BBC World Service reporting our raid. It seemed a long, long drag back to Wide Awake in Ascension Island. The adrenalin had gone and there was an awful lot of sea."

Sqn Ldr John Reeve, former Vulcan pilot

VULCAN

This delta-winged giant never fails to make an unforgettable impression upon the thousands of airshow spectators who witness its near vertical climb and wing-overs, as it is put through its paces by the Vulcan Display Flight.

VULCAN

The tail sting of the B-52G comprises four 0.50-inch machine guns. These are slaved to a fire control system which is operated by a crew member in the main crew department. Prior to the 'G' model, the tail gunner often flew the entire mission in the lonely 'office' in the tail of the B-52, and the only access to the flight deck was via an extremely long crawlway.

The distinctive shape of the Boeing B-52 Stratofortress. It first entered service in 1955 and is probably remembered best for its involvement in Vietnam during Linebacker 11 operations. The B-52 or 'BUFF' (big ugly fat f . . . !) will have the longest operational career of any military aircraft.

"Probably the oldest USAF combat aircaft still in front-line service, the B-52 is a hard act to follow. When it entered service in 1957 it was the logical successor to a long line of strategic bombers; few thought that it would still be around over 30 years later. Not only around, but still on 'active duty' with 'Buffs' taking part in the Gulf War.

The sight of a Buff streaming black smoke from the engines as it lumbers down the runway towards you is unforgettable, a little further on and the wing-tips get airborne . . . a few thousand feet more of runway and the rest of the beast rises from the ground – and sticks its nose down into that characteristic take-off attitude. As an aircraft to work on, the B-52 is a mix of modern high-tech electronics and good old-fashioned systems.

Over the years the B-52 has been updated and improved, and the G models we fly now are nothing like the early models. We still tote a massive bomb load, an awesome sight to witness when a Buff empties its load. When the B-52s finally retire it will be the end of an era. There is nothing else quite like them."

B-52G pilot, 42nd Bombardment Wing, Loring AFB, Maine

B-52

"The first time that I saw a B-I at an air display I was amazed at the way in which the pilot threw the aircraft around, starting with a tight turn straight after take-off. The final low level high-speed pass, with the wings fully swept back, was fantastic. My first thought was, how do I get this for my display! What makes the Lancer so special is the very advanced systems it carries, both for attack and defence. The weapon load is truly awesome, yet has little effect on the overall performance of the airplane. It is very much a crew operation; each of the specialists has a job to do in order to ensure that the mission is a success. Flying a display gives the crew a chance to show off the performance characteristics of the aircraft, and throwing such a big aircraft into tight manoeuvres always impresses the crowd.

Conceived as a strategic bomber to replace or at least supplement the aged B-52s, the B-I had a very on-off existence under various Presidencies. Given the go-ahead the long-delayed, and troublesome, programme at last saw deliveries to Strategic Air Command in 1985.

Although the B-I incorporates a number of stealth features, it is a pre-stealth technology aircraft and so its viability as a strategic bomber has been called into question. However, changing East-West relations, and the ever-rising costs of the B-2 stealth bomber, may well mean there is a long-term future for the B-I as the B-52s finally reach the end of their days."

Air display co-ordinator

The Rockwell International B-1 Lancer was designed as a strategic bomber to replace the aging B-52, until the futuristic B-2 'stealth' bomber came on the scene. The B-1 has, like the F-111, variable geometry wings.

B-1 LANCER

CHAPTER 5

OF BLADES & SMOKE

Diving out of the stolen car, the fugitive runs into the darkness. But he has failed to take account of the police helicopter's relentless pursuit and its ability to link up with the hunters on the ground. As the public address system booms out above him, he freezes; then the sweeping searchlight pinpoints him and, caught in the dazzling beam, he is helpless to escape the waiting ground unit.

In many operations the helicopter has an obvious advantage over conventional aircraft. It has almost unlimited mobility and can respond in minutes. As an executive transport, it can save time spent in traffic jams or waiting for scheduled flights – and time is money. And the helicopter has proved itself in wartime, from its early days as a vital backup, to the modern deadly weapon of attack, as seen in the Gulf.

Fixed wing aircraft have opened up the skies, but helicopters have opened the landmasses, islands and continents, remote or populated, with their power to take off and land vertically, to hover and move in any direction.

The latter end of the 20th century is the age of the helicopter. But it has been a late arrival in the transportation world. Throughout the ages man has tried to design an aircraft that can fly vertically. As early as 1483 Leonardo da Vinci made copious drawings and again in the 19th century plans were made to apply steam power to rotorcraft. But it was not until the advent of the gasoline engine that powered flight with all its connotations became a practical proposition.

The helicopter is sometimes described as a 'wingless' aircraft that obtains life and propulsion from overhead horizontally turning rotors. But the rotors of the helicopter fulfil the same functions as the wings of an aeroplane, with engine power turning the rotors into rotating wings. Because of this whirling wing an enormous amount of torque is generated, which wants to turn the helicopter in the opposite direction. This is countered by a small rotor on the tail of the craft which effectively pushes against the torque and stabilises the energies. This makes a very interesting form of powered flight. It has been described as like trying to keep your balance standing on a floating sphere.

When this technique is mastered, it gives an incredible degree of manoeuvrability and the ability to change direction at will.

Westland Gazelle HT2 of the Royal Navy Helicopter Display Team, the 'Sharks'.

ABOVE *The Russian Kamov Ka-32T* is a civilian version of the almost identical Ka-27 Helix B. The Ka-27 is operated by the Soviet Navy as an amphibious assault helicopter. Its primary role is the delivery of precision guided weapons and it operates from guided missile destroyers and carriers.

ABOVE RIGHT *The Polish PZL-Sokol (Falcon)* is a multipurpose utility helicopter which has an endurance time of over 4 hours using internal fuel. It can carry up to 12 passengers in its transport role, or as an air ambulance it carries 4 stretchers.

RIGHT *The Soviet Union's Mi-171* from the Mikhail Mil design bureau. This is another civilian version of a very successful military assault helicopter.

" The Soviet range of giant Mil helicopters still tends to be associated with Cold War days, with the sinister goggle-eyed air intakes of their gas turbine engines and gunship weaponry and pylons for rocket pods. Added to these, they have formidable world records in size, endurance and payload.

I flew in the 24-seat helicopter on several occasions and found that the roof mounted engines allowed much more space for cargo and passengers. It was rather like riding in a country bus, with the seats facing inwards and the cargo, anything from sacks of grain to chickens or packets of medication, down the centre. The seats were basic and you had to crane your neck to see the breathtaking scenery so near below. They flew by the seat of their pants, mountain hopping as if on a tightrope and every landing a blind challenge in a large cloud of dust from rotor action. They were a breath of fresh air in a fraught world."

International aid worker in Ethiopia

The Boeing Vertol CH-47 Chinook *or 'Wocca' as it is known in the UK. This is a twin Tandem Rotor helicopter (TTR) and is designed so that the contra-rotating rotors counteract the torque generated. This does away with the need for a tail rotor.*

"The first time I worked underneath a Chinook we had to get a large piece of equipment off a man-made fort off Portsmouth. The older and wiser members of the team stayed on the mainland to take off the load while the rest of us riggers, none of whom had operated under a Chinook before, rigged the load, decided we'd got it right and called in the aircraft.

In 30 seconds the whole scheme was a tatty heap, blown to bits by the rotor downwash, and our clothes were ripped off. Meanwhile the rest of the party were having a field day – the drop-off point looked down on a nudist beach.

A Chinook can lift another Chinook. It's the only helicopter that can lift its own weight. But it's capable of blowing a container off a ship and has to be treated with the greatest respect. We dress up warmly against the chill factor from the downwash.

Much of our work is with crash recoveries and we are on standby for any disaster to deliver underslung loads of relief supplies. Lifting aircraft is very sensitive because of their soft skins. We often get called on to deliver an unusual load such as mountain rescue huts, an extension to a TV mast on Mount Olympus in Cyprus, kidney dialysis machines, or a weather station on the island of Rona."

Chief Petty Officer Bill Hookins RN, Joint Air Transport Establishment

CHINOOK

TOP *Flying instructor Kevin Sutton* demonstrating the Bell 47 'Sioux'.
ABOVE LEFT *A Westland Gazelle HT3* of the Royal Navy 'Sharks' display team.
ABOVE *Westland Whirlwind HAS.*
BOTTOM LEFT *Westland Lynx.*
OPPOSITE PAGE *Alouette 111s* of the Royal Netherlands Air Force Helicopter Display Team, 'The Grasshoppers'.

CHAPTER 6

DISPLAY TEAMS

"**L**adies and Gentlemen . . . from your right, the Royal Air Force Aerobatic Display Team . . . The RED ARROWS!" This announcement heralds a visual (and aural) display of synchronised flying by 10 front line trainer/combat jets weaving in and out, performing intricate sequences and passes, that is stunning in its execution.

This team is but one of a handful of highly skilled squadrons that exist to perform to the public at airshows around the world. They give the spectators a taste of what can be achieved when men and machines work in harmony, as part of a team . . . as one. The attributes combined with this performance represent the tools that are required for a life in today's airforces.

The Red Arrows are the 'jewel in the crown' of the RAF and are actively involved in promoting the Air Force to dozens of countries each year. The same goes for the 'Thunderbirds' (USAF), 'Team Aguila' (Spanish Air Force), 'Freece Tricolori' (Italian Air Force), 'Patrouille de France' (French Air Force) and many others worldwide.

Display teams, by definition, are not confined to the fast jet community; there are teams who fly WW 2 pistoned classics, or purpose built modern aerobatic machines like the Lexus, CAP and SU-26, whose performances are breathtaking.

Witnessing a display team in action, whether it be jets, pistons or parachutes, is a special moment as it more often than not heralds the beginning or end of the show. The smell of hot-dogs and aviation fuel, cut grass and candyfloss, and the tannoy's metallic call combine in a unique sensation of excitement that is the airshow's greatest thrill.

ABOVE & OPPOSITE *The Royal Air Force Aerobatic Display Team, the 'Red Arrows',* flying BAe Hawk T1As. The Hawk is an advanced two seat trainer and weapons trainer, as well as an air defence fighter in its war role.

"At one airshow, at a briefing, a commander got up eventually and said, 'Gentlemen, let's thrill the ignorant, impress the knowledgeable and scare no one!' That really spells out what you want from an airshow. Putting together a flying display, you've got to ask yourself, what would you as a member of the public like to see? With the modern jet aircraft, when they come through they make a lot of noise and it's basically a loop, a wingover, a roll and that is the sequence. After you've had about three high-speed jets on the trot it gets a bit boring, so what you want to do is vary the menu. Of course, everybody wants to see modern aircraft. From the Gulf War you would want a Buccaneer, Tornado, Jaguar, the American A-10, but also if you can feed in the more historic aircraft it's going to be a photographer's paradise. The last one I organised ran for 7 hours 15 minutes non-stop, with 30 seconds to a minute between items.

At a show like Brize Norton, on a good day you would expect a crowd of between 28,000 and 35,000. From the takings, after paying out for St John's Ambulance, crowd control barriers, extra police, etc., hopefully we have a nice sum to give to the RAF Benevolent Fund and a little left for the start of next year's initial outgoings.

The very first show I ever organised, we were unfortunate enough to have a fatal. It did teach me one thing – from that time onwards, every show I organised, I had a video camera running at all times. If anything happened, it could be seen by the investigators, frame by frame, to help them in their work."

Sqn Ldr Pete 'Jimmy' Jewel, airshow organiser

ABOVE *'Team Aguila', the Spanish Air Force Display Team,* in their CASA Aviojets performing at the International Air Tattoo.
LEFT *The Toyota Display Team* led by British Aerobatic Champion Nigel Lamb in his Lexus Extra 300. Nigel has held this record for five consecutive years. To his left and right are the team's two Pitts Special 300s.

ABOVE **Alpha Jets** of the French Air Force Aerobatic Team 'Patrouille de France', being led back to the flight line after a display.

RIGHT **A mirrored pair demonstration** from 'Team Aguila' the Spanish Air Force Display Team. This set piece is performed by many display teams worldwide, but is nevertheless a highly skilled manoeuvre.

Hawker Hunter F58s of the Swiss Air Force Display Team, 'Patrouille Suisse'.

General Dynamics F-16A Fighting Falcons, of the USAF Display Team, 'The Thunderbirds', during their European tour of 1991.

The Royal Air Force Parachute Display Team, 'The Falcons'.
LEFT *The Falcons exiting their prime jump platform, the C-130 Hercules. During the Gulf War, when the Hercs were operational, the Falcons transferred to the Hawker Siddeley Andover E3.* RIGHT *The Falcons in freefall over the home of the Queen's Flight, RAF Benson.*

ABOVE *The Falcons under canopy* and positioning for their unique canopy stack spiral.
LEFT *Hawker Siddeley Andover E3* returns to the display pan after despatching the Falcons.

"The Falcons have three display patterns. Our latest display is our 'mid-show' from 8,000 to 4,000ft, involving a freefall formation of ten in contact, followed by a bomb burst effect before we open our parachutes. In each case the canopy stack is similar. When the weather permits we aim to do a split stack spiral with the bottom five and top five spiralling in opposite directions before meeting up again. At 1,000ft the whole stack spirals in the same direction.

The other two are the 'high show' from 12,000 to 8,000ft and the 'low show' from the Andover at 4,000 to 2,800ft, clearing the aircraft in tight formation then opening the parachute together on the coach's signal.

The team is reduced from 15 to 13 for 1992 – three on the ground and ten jumpers. Our new parachute, the 'Fury', is a seven cell square parachute similar to the previous 'XL Cloud' but more sporty. It has a square reserve as well – better over built-up areas as it's more steerable.

Because of the Gulf commitments of the C-130 Hercules the Andover was made available to us for the 1991 season. We had two full crews and an Andover from 115 squadron. It was good having the same crews, they got to know us and welcomed the change from their normal calibration tasks. It's more comfortable than the Hercules but not so spectacular for the public. The drawbacks of a smaller aircraft are that it won't take our vehicles and it's slower. Going abroad takes longer with more overnight stops.

The Andover needs a lot of trimming. We leave the aircraft in pairs and as I'm in one of the last pairs I've noticed how the aircraft nosedives. It can be quite difficult to get out.

I've been three and a half years with No1 Parachute Training School and this is my second year on the team. You need to be competent and it's great for learning to become a good free faller and then to progress to more demanding military jobs. It's fair to say that when the cloudbase is very low there's an element of apprehension.

The worst scenario is if one has a malfunction and has to cut away the main parachute and operate the reserve, always a frightening moment. When it happens that man can't take part in the display but has to fend for himself and find somewhere to land."

Flt Lt Rhys Cowsill, team leader,
The Falcons

CHAPTER 7
BACK TO LIFE

The tropical sunlight and changing weather conditions of 40 years had totally stripped the paint off the wrecked hulk of the Lockheed P-38 Lightning, leaving its bare metal skin exposed. Its canopy cracked and yellowed, its propellers bent and wings broken, the fuselage played host to the lush foliage, which crept through every possible opening in the airframe.

Images like this can still be found in the inhospitable mountains and swamps of the islands of the South Pacific, where 40 years ago powerful war birds battled in aerial combat for supremacy of the skies.

Witnessing a wreck like this, you could never imagine that one day it would again fly, but they can and do, thanks to the dedicated teams whose life is Aviation Restoration (or Archaeology as it is sometimes called). The sheer logistics, legal hurdles and cost of locating and removing a wreck from the other side of the world are enormous, not to mention the subsequent restoration to flying condition. The Beaufighter project (left) is estimated to be a 5 year rebuild! This mammoth task relies on an army of helpers, many of whom have a multiplicity of skills. Without these dedicated people (mostly volunteers who give up literally years of their time), the majority of vintage aircraft on today's airshow circuits would simply not exist.

All the surface wrecks from 'Fortress Europe' were removed as and when they crashed during the two wars. Other countries such as Australia and the Soviet Union have vast tracts of land that have often never seen a human footprint. Due to more and more 4-wheel drive expeditions and private aircraft 'adventure' holidays, airframes are now being discovered, often in perfect condition, where the pilots either got lost or ran out of fuel, or both.

Not all restoration revolves around crash sites. Aircraft have quite often been found stored and forgotten in a barn for 30-odd years, or others are a composite rebuild, a hybrid constructed from a number of different airframes – whichever way it happens, the end result is that we can once again witness these sleek flying machines, performing in the element for which they were designed, having been brought 'back to life'.

The beginning of a long rebuild. In about five years these engines will power a restored Bristol Beaufighter which at present is a battered hulk. The Beaufighter is a recent acquisition by the Fighter Collection.

"Our philosophy is to restore an aircraft to exactly how it was, with all the atmosphere of a WW 1 or WW 2 aeroplane. If you deviate from the true concept you can wind up with a shell that is almost too perfect. It may be ideal for the customer but bear no resemblance to the genuine aircraft. I've seen pre-war touring aircraft look immaculate with high gloss paint, though not remotely like they used to be. At the end of the day it's got to fly and should look as if it has never been restored, just a beautifully kept original aircraft. We are the custodians and these aircraft are here to pass on, with the feel and knowledge of time. Any deviation and 20 years later how it should have been is forgotten and what is in the aircraft is accepted as original. To my mind, to install visible modern avionics into the cockpit when the exterior is meant to look like an original WW 2 aircraft is sacrilege except for reasons of safety.

There are two entities in aircraft restoration, the private owner who does home restoration and the professional contractor like ourselves. A very broad knowledge of antique aircraft is as important as documentation. We often find that WW 2 aircraft were issued with a set of documents when they were manufactured. When it was found that they didn't work they made modifications but didn't record them. They got caught out and so can we. It could be dangerous.

We've done a number of massive renovations of classic aircraft, WW 1 and WW 2 fighters such as the Spitfire, the Westland Lysander, 1930s touring aircraft, trainers, a couple of Mosquitos and also a lot of replicas which are genuine fakes."

Tony Bianchi, 'The Blue Max Collection'

Some of the projects (flying and static) currently in progress in the Royal New Zealand Air Force museum at RNZAF base Wigram. This museum was one of the first to use theatrical lighting for its exhibits.
RIGHT *PBY Catalina* in background, De Havilland Mosquito in foreground.
BELOW *The RNZAF museum Wigram.*
OPPOSITE PAGE *Various stages in the restoration of a WW 2 Lockheed Ventura.* Other aircraft awaiting restoration include a Bristol Freighter, F4U Corsair, TBM Avenger and Lockheed Lodestar.

ABOVE **A very rare Hawker Tempest 2** being restored at Duxford, unfortunately a static restoration. However, the standard of work on this project by the Fighter Collection means that the machine will be in flying condition. The Tempest is an ex-Indian Air Force example.

RIGHT **The Airspeed Ambassador** first flew in 1947 and was designed as a short-haul airliner. Due to development problems, the Ambassador was superseded by the Vickers Viscount, so only 23 of the type were ever produced. This particular machine flew with BEA, Dan Air, and the Royal Jordanian Air Force. It is currently being restored at the Imperial War Museum's Duxford location in Cambridgeshire.

Nick Grey of 'The Fighter Collection' in 'Candyman', a P51D. *The collection is without a doubt the most prolific warbird operation in Europe, comprising such types as the F64 Hellcat, F4F Wildcat, P-51D, Spitfires, F84 Bearcat, P-63 Kingcobra, P-38 Lightning, Hurricane, Corsair, P-47 Thunderbolt and P-40 Kittyhawk, Sea Fury and Yak-3, to name but a few.*

"Why become an aircraft restoration enthusiast? It's the love of old aircraft and the great satisfaction and thrill of seeing them fly on the airshow circuit and saying to yourself – 'I had a hand in that!' I am a member of the Sandy Topen five-man Vintage Aircraft Team. It's been restoring old fighters at Cranfield for 14 years. Now we've moved to Bruntingthorpe in Leicestershire – a major operation conveying the wrecks and spares!

All our personally owned restored aircraft fly on the airshow circuit. It is Sandy's greatest dream to see our Miles Stewart flying again. It arrived at Cranfield completely wrecked after flying at too steep an angle, a lack of airflow causing a vacuum in the air intake. We are restoring it with the aid of a sheet metal worker.

We have a huge store of Venom and Vampire spares. Some of our more recent restorations have included an ex Swiss built Mk 1 Venom (a major rebuild with everything overhauled except the interior cockpit) and a T11 Vampire (entailing a complete strip – it had been on static display and was in a tatty condition), both owned by Don Woods, and also a Jet Provost.

Some of the most interesting aircraft we've had in the past have been a Fokker triplane, an Army Auster, a Mustang, the remains of an FB8 Gunbus built for the film *Shout at the Devil* and a T33 Shooting Star – all built to fly again."

Alan Paul, member of the Vintage Aircraft Team

ACKNOWLEDGEMENTS

The production of this book has been a major undertaking in terms of people involved. For all their generous help and enthusiasm towards AIRSHOW I would like to mention some by name.

IMPERIAL WAR MUSEUM, DUXFORD
Stephen and Nick Grey of the Fighter Collection.
Captain Keith Sissons, Sqn Ldr Pete Jewel and Elly Sallingboe of B-17 Preservation Ltd.

Carol Stearn, with thanks for the many 'live sides'.

INTERNATIONAL AIR TATTOO
Sue Bushell.

RAF FININGLEY
Flt Lt Ken Delve.

RAF LYNEHAM
Sqn Ldr Harry Burgoyne, Flt Lt Howard Elliot,
Sqn Ldr Al Holman from 242 OCU.
Flt Lt Ted Querzani.

RNZAF BASE, WIGRAM
Sqn Ldr John Berry.

THE SQUADRON
Anthony Hutton & The Squadron.

USAFE (United States Air Forces Europe) UPPER HEYFORD
77th TFS & 42nd ECS.
Richard Coley.

THE BLUE MAX COLLECTION
Tony Bianchi for all his help and enthusiasm and for the privilege of seeing his classic flying machines air to air, and for the initiation to the Stampe. Jonathon Whaley, film & stunt pilot, who, as an ex-F4 pilot, flew the Chipmunk camera ship with feeling!

On the production side of things my warmest thanks must go to Molly O'Loughlin White, for her words and 'music' and who knew exactly what I was looking for.
To Barry Roberts for appearing 'out of the blue'.
Lindsay Peacock, David Donald and Paul Jackson for facts and figures at the last minute.
Gary Numan and Tony & Beryl Webb for the great foreword.
Jerry Burman for all his help . . . and patience during the production of AIRSHOW.
Richard Leonard, assistant extraordinaire, whose presence on the numerous flight decks was always a source of inspiration.

Lastly, to my wife Nic for being there . . . I promise no more airshows (well, maybe)!

PHOTOGRAPHIC NOTES

All the images in AIRSHOW were taken with a Nikon F4s or F3. Film stock was Fujichrome 50 / 100 / 3200. Lenses ranged from a 16mm fisheye to a 600mm mirror.

Since arriving in the UK from his native New Zealand in 1980, Jon Davison has built up a reputation for being an outstanding colour photographer. His use of light and his sympathy with his subject matter make him an internationally respected lensman. He has illustrated many books on aviation and travel including: *Upper Heyford* (the F-111), *Red On Go* (military parachuting), *Fat Albert* (the C-130 Hercules), *Oxford, Cambridge, Bath, Yorkshire, Mexico's Yucatan,* and many others. Over half of these publications Jon has designed and produced himself. His photographs are represented worldwide by The Image Bank (TIB) in New York.

BACKGROUND IMAGE **Fairey Flycatcher.**